Labrador Retrievers

NIKKI MOUSTAKI

Labrador Retrievers
An Interpet Book

Project Team
Editor: Stephanie Fornino
Copy Editor: Joann Woy
Interior Design: Leah Lococo Ltd. and Stephanie Krautheim
Design Layout: Tilly Grassa

First Published in UK by
Interpet Publishing
Vincent Lane
Dorking
Surrey
RH4 3YX

ISBN: 978 1 84286 158 5

©2006 T.F.H. Publications, Inc.

Printed and bound in China

This book has been published with the intent to provide accurate and authoritative information in regard to the subject matter within. While every precaution has been taken in preparation of this book, the author and publisher expressly disclaim responsibility for any errors, omissions, or adverse effects arising from the use or application of the information contained herein. The techniques and suggestions are used at the reader's discretion and are not to be considered a substitute for veterinary care. If you suspect a medical problem consult your vet.

v.interpet.co.uk

Table of Contents

Chapter 1

Why I Adore My
Labrador Retriever

It is no surprise that the Labrador Retriever is one of the most popular breeds in the world. In fact, this intelligent, gentle, kind, and reliable family pet and sporting companion leads the top of the list of the Kennel Club (KC) and American Kennel Club (AKC) registries.

The Lab is an incredibly adaptable dog, ideal for both city and rural living, for family life or the single dog lover, and he is just as reliable retrieving game on land as he is in the water. This breed is a full-service gundog, bred to flush game as well as retrieve it. He is a member of the Gundog Group in the KC, and the Sporting Group in the AKC, although he doesn't need to hunt to be content in the average home. Hardy games of fetch, afternoons of swimming in the pool or at the local pond, and canine sports like obedience and agility allow the house Lab to do what he does best—please his owners.

The Lab is an incredibly adaptable dog who is reliable retrieving game both on land and in the water.

Congratulations on your decision to discover more about this wonderful breed. In this book, you will learn about how to outfit your Lab with everything he needs when you bring him home, how to properly feed him, the right kind of training to implement, health issues particular to the breed, how to travel safely with your Lab, and much more. Welcome to the world of Labrador Retrievers!

A Little Lab History

The Labrador Retriever began as a breed in Newfoundland, not in Labrador, and was likely named by his early British fanciers who lumped together the two distinct geographical locations. His predecessors were the Newfoundland dogs, and like other gundog breeds, the Lab was developed to have characteristics that his human companions found useful. In this case, the breed may have had its origins in the fishing villages of the St. John's

district of Newfoundland in the 1600s, where fishermen used dogs to help haul in the catch. They needed dogs with a dense, water-repellent coat that wouldn't soak up excess water or ball up with ice. The dogs they used became known for their tireless working abilities.

As life changed in the villages, so did the "St. John's dog," as he became a hunting and retrieving companion. British settlers brought the prized dogs back to England in the early 1800s, where the breed was refined and maintained by the English gentry and named the Labrador Retriever.

The Lab in England

Once in England, the early Labs were refined to improve their hunting and retrieving abilities. The Lab soon began to take on the look of the dog we know today, with his sleek, water-resistant coat and "otter" tail (a round tail that is thick at the root and tapered to the end, with the hair parted along the underside).

The Labrador Retriever flourished in England and was officially recognised by the English Kennel Club in 1903.

The Lab in the United States

Most of the Labradors in the United States today are descended from English Labradors who were brought over after World War I. Some slight differences are apparent between the American and English Labrador. English

The First Labrador Retriever

The first Labrador Retriever was brought to England from Newfoundland by the Earl of Malmesbury in the early nineteenth century. It was the Earl who coined the name "Labrador" and encouraged the Lab to become a favoured gundog in England.

Labradors are generally slightly smaller and stockier than the American type, but both national kennel clubs maintain virtually the same breed standard. Neither the American Kennel Club nor the United Kennel Club (UKC) differentiates between the two types. In 1917, the AKC recognised and registered the Lab, and the love affair with this dog took off in earnest.

Today, the Labrador is used as a gundog, household companion, assistance dog, and detection dog. Labs are eager to retrieve anything, and they have a "soft" mouth, able to fetch a fallen duck, for example, without leaving teeth marks or causing further damage to the bird. They also have excellent vision and

The Expert Knows

Lab Colours

Although we know Labrador Retrievers as being black, chocolate, or yellow, they were originally bred to be just black. The first yellow Labrador did not come into existence until 1899. Chocolate was the last colour to develop and was not immediately accepted into the KC breed standard. It is still the least popular colour for the Labrador Retriever.

scenting abilities; it has been said that their keen sense of smell is twice that of some other dog breeds. The Lab's webbed feet (the breed has skin between the toes) make him an excellent swimmer.

General Appearance

The following basic description represents the "ideal" Lab who might participate in dog shows, where physical appearance is of utmost concern. For the average companion Lab, beauty standards aren't this strict. The most motley of Labs can make wonderful pets.

Height and Weight

The ideal height for a Labrador can be anywhere from 21½ (55 cm) to 22½ (57 cm) inches tall at the withers. Weight is not stipulated in the KC standard but averages between 55 (24.9 kg) and 80 pounds (36.3 kg).

Head

The Labrador's head should be wide but not overly so in proportion to the body. The top of the head and muzzle should be the same length and parallel to one another. A brow separates the two, with slight brow ridges. The Lab should not have much by way of cheeks or jowls that hang down. Instead, his lips should curve back toward the throat.

Teeth

The teeth should be straight, with the top teeth falling in front of the bottom teeth just far enough that they do not touch, forming a scissor bite.

Eyes

The Labrador's eyes should be medium sized and set far apart; they should be neither deep set nor protruding. Eye colour depends on coat colour. For black and yellow Labs, eyes should be brown, as should the skin around the eyes. For chocolate Labs, eye colour can be brown or hazel, and the skin around the eye should be chocolate in colour, matching the rest of the dog.

His webbed feet make the Lab an excellent swimmer.

Nose

The nose of a black or yellow Lab should be black. A chocolate Lab should have a chocolate nose. On some Labs, the colour of the nose is slightly lighter than the rest of the coat.

Ears

The ears of the Labrador sit low and far back on the head. The ears stay close to the head and are neither too big nor too heavy.

Neck, Back, and Shoulders

The neck of the Labrador should be long enough for him to retrieve game effortlessly. The dog's back should be straight and level, his ribcage widening slightly from the waist to the chest. An animal who has a too-narrow ribcage or is too barrel chested can result in awkward and improper movement and lack of stamina. Like the Lab's back, his underside is straight and virtually level, not curving upward as dramatically into a waist as in some other breeds.

The setting of a Lab's shoulders affects how he looks and walks. Ideally, the shoulders should form a 90-degree angle with the upper leg.

The shoulders should be laid back and allow the dog to have a far forward reach. The shoulder and the upper leg should be the same length.

Front and Back Legs

The front legs of the Labrador should be straight and the bones of medium

SENIOR DOG TIP

The Lab Lifespan

The average lifespan for the Labrador is 12 to 13 years. Although the ageing process varies from dog to dog, Labradors are usually considered veterans at nine or ten years of age and may begin to experience declining health at this time.

thickness, not too delicate or too thick. The elbows and feet should point straight ahead and not turn in or out.

Like the front legs, the Lab's back legs should be straight and parallel. The hind legs are powerful, with short hocks and well-muscled thighs. The angle of the rear legs should mirror the angle of the front legs. The hocks and stifle are strong. The toes should be strong and arched, and the dog's pads should be cushiony. Toes on the rear feet should reach slightly behind the rump when the dog is standing.

Tail

One of the most distinguishing characteristics of the Labrador is his "otter" tail. It should be thicker at the base, gradually tapering to the end, and come to the length of the dog's hock when lying flat. The Lab's coat covers the tail but does not feather. When the dog moves, the tail should follow the lines of his back. The tail is not docked.

Gait

A Lab should move effortlessly and easily. The back should be level, the legs parallel and moving with a free range of motion. Movements should not be choppy or awkward but rather graceful and natural.

Coat

The Labrador's coat, which can be chocolate, yellow, or black, is made up of an undercoat and outercoat. Both coats are short and straight, and together they are very dense. The undercoat is softer and water resistant, protecting the dog when swimming or hunting in other rough or watery terrains. The outercoat is stiff to the touch but sleek to the eye. Some dogs' may have a wave down their backs, but the coat should not have any curl. Some Labs may have a white spot on their chest.

Other colours, textures, or lengths of hair are not characteristic of the Lab. No such thing as a "silver" Lab exists, although you may see them

The Labrador's coat can be black, chocolate, or yellow.

advertised. These dogs are often crossed with Weimaraners or other breeds, so be wary if you encounter a breeder touting colours other than black, yellow, or chocolate.

Temperament and Personality

The temperament of the Labrador is perhaps his finest feature. A long list of complimentary characteristics is used to describe this breed: loyal, trustworthy, kind-hearted, patient, intelligent, and loving, to name just a few.

A testament to the Lab's great temperament is the fact that this breed is used widely as an assistance dog for the blind, people in wheelchairs, seizure-alert dogs, and as therapy dogs. They are typically used as search-and-rescue and detection dogs, both jobs that require close contact with the public.

Activity Level

Labs are sporting dogs who are able to run for miles (km) and play for hours at games of fetch. A Lab who is confined to a small space or who isn't given enough exercise can become overweight and even destructive in an effort to find a way to get rid of his excess energy. Play vigorously with your Lab for at least half an hour a day. If

FAMILY-FRIENDLY TIP

Labs and Kids: Are They a Good Match?

The Labrador Retriever makes a wonderful family companion and is superb with children. The breed is characteristically gentle and friendly, and aggression toward children is very rare. At the same time, children should learn to appropriately interact with the Lab, and young children need adult supervision with dogs at all times.

years of age, for the most part Labs are patient and offer a high level of attention to detail and efficiency.

Environment

The Lab is happiest when he's on a shoot, hike, long walk, or playing fetch in a garden. A rural or suburban environment is perfect for this active dog. However, the Lab is a highly adaptable dog, and he will do very well with city life as long as his owner is able to give him long walks and romps in the park.

Family Suitability

Generally speaking, Labradors have a solid and good-natured temperament and are well-behaved when trained

you're a couch potato, don't worry—just toss a ball, and your dog should bring it right back! Playing fetch in a lake or pool is especially fun for a Lab. Be careful, however, of the Lab who becomes too excited or exercises too intensely. Underlying medical conditions can cause the dog to collapse. Also, make sure that your dog has water at all times and doesn't become overheated.

Labs can be stubborn, but for the most part, they aim to please. They are enthusiastic but not overly hyper, and although some individuals might be considered kind of "clowny," especially those under three

Most Labs are great family dogs who make ideal companions for children.

properly and given the proper care. A typical Labrador loves the company of people. They are great for families and make ideal companions for children. However, as with every dog breed, individual exceptions occur. Every so often, a Lab may be either shy or aggressive, although these traits are atypical of the breed.

Because they are bred to serve humans, Labs prefer home life and the company of their families.

Trainability

This breed is definitely motivated by food, but that just makes it all that much easier to train. Evidence of the Lab's trainability is clear in his role as a reliable assistance dog, search-and-

Celebrity Lab Lovers

Celebs love Labs, too! Minnie Driver owns a Labrador, and Gwyneth Paltrow was very fond of her Lab, Holden. Rupert Everett owned a Lab named Moise. Steve Martin is the proud owner of a yellow Lab named Roger. Labradors even cross political lines. Bill Clinton owned a chocolate Lab named Buddy, and Dick Cheney has two Labs, Jackson and Davey. Lab mixes are also popular—Drew Barrymore and Matthew McConaughey both own Labrador/Chow mixes.

rescue dog, and detection dog. They also excel in obedience and field trials. The Lab can easily handle the everyday commands of an average pet owner, like *sit*, *stay*, *come*, and *down*.

The Lab is the UK's favourite dog for good reason, as you can see. He has everything you could ask for in a medium- to large-sized dog, including brains, trainability, companionability, and a lot more. It's impossible not to love a Lab!

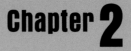

Chapter 2

The Stuff of
Everyday Life

Whether you've adopted a Lab puppy or adult, you're going to need some supplies to get started in your adventure as a new Lab owner. You can stick with the basics or go wild with a lot of the fun dog accessories on the market today. In this chapter, you'll get a rundown of the basic stuff you will need when you bring your Lab home, as well as an idea of some of the other items that make living with a dog much easier.

Bed

Your Lab's bed should be large enough for him to curl up on. It should also be soft and comfy, and most important, be durable and washable. Even if you allow your Lab to sleep in your bed, he will need a place of his own to lie down on when you ask him to stay out of the way or when he needs a nap. If you buy a good-quality bed from the start, you won't have to replace it as often, but expect to replace most beds every few years.

Collar

Your Lab needs a collar on at all times while you're in the process of training. However, he should not wear a collar (or anything else) when he's confined to a crate or when you're not home to supervise him. The collar could get caught on something, and he could panic, leading to injury or worse.

Flat Buckle Collar

All dogs should have a flat, nylon buckle collar with an ID tag attached to it. You will probably have to purchase two collars as your Lab grows, a small one when he's a puppy and then an adjustable collar once your Lab is a few months old. Don't let the collar get too tight—if you can put two fingers snugly between the collar and the dog's neck, it fits correctly. You can substitute a flat or rolled leather collar as your dog's main collar after he's trained, but remember that leather can smell if it

Setting Up a Schedule

If dogs were human, they would live with a handheld organiser glued to one paw. They love their schedule and will hold you to it by bringing you the lead or knocking around the food bowl. Puppies, especially, need a rigorous schedule because they have to relieve themselves often. Feed your puppy as often as your vet suggests (usually twice a day), and take him out to relieve himself first thing in the morning and then every two to three hours until bedtime. Your adult dog will need to relieve himself at least three times a day—morning, afternoon, and night-time, and he will appreciate an extra walk or playtime in the garden if you can provide it.

gets wet consistently. Nylon has the advantage of being washable, and it comes in fashionable colours and patterns.

Head Halter

The head halter is also designed for dogs who like to pull on the lead. It fits snugly over the head and muzzle, and turns the dog's head towards the pressure on the lead (that's you, if you're holding it) when he pulls. Soon, the dog realises that when he pulls, he gets uncomfortably turned around. This is a nice quick fix for some dogs, but training is more effective in the long run. Many dogs react poorly to the head halter, at least initially, by trying to get it off, which defeats the purpose of helping the dog learn to walk nicely on the lead.

All dogs should have a flat, nylon buckle collar.

Harness

A body harness is fine for the Lab who doesn't pull on the lead during a walk. A Lab who likes swimming while boating will need a harness so that it's easier to grab him out of the water. One body harness features a clip at the dog's chest rather than at the shoulders, which acts similarly to the head halter by turning the dog around when he pulls. This is a good option for someone who needs a little extra control on walks and has a dog who isn't comfortable with the head halter.

Choke Collars

Some people use nylon or chain-link choke collars for a stubborn Lab who is pulling on the lead. You are better off finding a way to train your Lab out of this behaviour than to put a choke collar on your dog. Positive reinforcement training may take longer, but it is much more effective than any choke collar on the market.

Dog Sitters and Dog Walkers

If you can't provide an afternoon walk because you work outside of the home all day, look into using a dog sitter or dog walker. A dog sitter will come to your home, let the dog out and play with him. A dog walker, on the other hand, comes into your home and takes your dog out, usually for an hour. Look into each option carefully, and speak with other clients to make sure that your dog will be properly cared for.

The Stuff of Everyday Life

Crate

A crate is not a cage or a prison. Dogs are denning animals who prefer to rest in dark, confined places where they feel safe. (This is why you'll often see your Lab reclining under the coffee table or in a dark corner.) It is designed to safely contain a dog when he needs some downtime, when you're not home, and when you're travelling. Even if you aren't going to use the crate on a daily basis, you should get your dog used to being inside it anyway. Even if you're not going to confine the dog to the crate regularly, have him use the crate as a bed so that, if you do have to enclose him in it for his own safety or because someone visiting your home is afraid of dogs, he will comply without so much as a woof.

There are three types of crates to look for, and each has its own benefits:

1. *Plastic crate:* Crates made of moulded plastic are durable, lightweight, easy to clean, and most are airline-approved.

2. *Wire crate:* Wire crates allow for good ventilation, give the dog a great view, and fold down for easy storage and transportation, but they are not airline-approved.

3. *Decorator crate:* Decorator crates come in a variety of materials, including wicker and wood, and are designed to fit nicely into any décor. These types of crates are better for the dog who is already crate trained and used to being confined.

A pen is ideal for confining your Lab outdoors.

Along with the crate, invest in a crate pad, usually made of an acrylic fleecy material. You can also use a flat dog bed or even an old blanket or towels in the bottom to make it comfy.

The crate should be large enough for the dog to stand up in comfortably and turn around with ease, but no larger. The dog should not have enough space to relieve himself inside the crate and then use another corner for sleeping. The crate shouldn't be used for mealtimes, either. It is a place where the dog settles in for a nice bone chew and a nap. Because the Lab is a large dog, look for a crate that has dividing panels so that your puppy can grow with his crate, and you don't have to invest in several crates as the dog grows.

In Chapter 6, you will receive step-by-step instructions on crate training as an effective form of housetraining, as well as a way to keep a young Lab from destroying your furniture while you're not supervising him. For now, put the crate on your list of must-have dog supplies.

Exercise Pen

An "ex-pen," short for exercise pen, is a series of gates locked together to form a barrier that confines your dog to a certain area. You can use an ex-pen inside the house or outdoors. Most are expandable, and you can buy as many sections of the gate as you need to

FAMILY-FRIENDLY TIP

Should Children Care for the Family Dog?

Labs and kids go together like peanut butter and jelly, but it's up to the adults in the home to provide the dog with proper care. Kids, even teenagers, should not be solely responsible for a dog. Of course, caring for the dog can be built into the child's list of chores, but please supervise any feeding, watering, or grooming to make sure that it's done right—or that it's done at all!

create an exercise area suitable for you and your dog. For Labs, make sure that the panels are at least 36 inches (91.4 cm) high, or the dog might climb or jump out.

If the ex-pen is used as the dog's primary confinement area outside the house, make sure that it is large enough to house a crate and still allow the dog to relieve himself at the other end of the confined area. Put toys and a water dish inside the pen, a soft bed inside the crate, and make sure that your dog isn't wearing a collar.

The Stuff of Everyday Life

Stainless steel bowls are durable, lightweight, and hygienic.

Food and Water Bowls

Ideally, purchase bowls made of stainless steel. Plastic bowls are fine temporarily, but they can become scratched, and bacteria will eventually grow in the crevices. Ceramic bowls are often designed with home décor in mind, but the glaze can craze and crack, and ceramic is much easier to break during regular cleaning. Stainless steel bowls will last the life of your dog, are lightweight, and come in all shapes and sizes.

The size of the bowl doesn't matter much, as long as the dog is getting his share of food. Lab puppies will need smaller bowls, graduating to larger bowls as they get older. The water dish should be unable to be tipped and have a nonskid surface on the bottom. Labs like to play in water, and you might have an individual who thinks it's fun to paw all the water out of his dish. With a heavy, non-skid bowl, you will be able to prevent the dish from tipping or skidding across the kitchen.

If your Lab spends time in the garden, provide him with another water dish outside. One type of water dispenser attaches to your garden hose and will provide your Lab with fresh water all the time. In the winter, make sure that the water bowl doesn't freeze over—your Lab can't drink ice. In this case, you can buy a self-heating water bowl that will keep the water from freezing.

Fill the water dish with fresh water at least twice a day. Keep water available at all times. Wash food dishes with warm, soapy water after each meal.

Gate

A baby gate can be used to confine the Lab to a specific area of the house, like the kitchen or laundry room, or to keep the dog away from a place you don't want him to enter, like an immaculate living room, the top of a stairwell, or the dining

The Expert Knows

ID
For Your Lab

Obviously you hope you will never lose your Labrador, but it is essential to be prepared for all eventualities. Your Labrador must carry some form of ID, which can be on his collar, or it can be a permanent form of ID, such as a microchip. Better still, your Lab should have both forms of ID.

room during dinner time. Baby gates are either tension-mounted or are installed with hardware inside a doorway. Get a gate that is at least 36 inches (91.4 cm) high, and invest in a high-quality gate from the start, because the less expensive ones tend to break more easily.

Identification

ID tags are critical and should be worn any time your dog is outdoors, even in your escape-proof garden. The ID tag should be made of plastic or metal and engraved with your dog's name (include your last name) and your current phone numbers. You can order them online or even have them made on the spot at many pet stores.

In the UK, all dogs are required to carry some form of identification. If your dog is picked up by the police or by a dog warden and does not have ID, you face paying a fine.

If your Lab has a medical condition, you can use a more detailed ID tag, which could also include the telephone number of your vet. Having your vet's telephone number is also useful if your dog is involved in an accident or injured.

Sometimes, an ID tag or collar can come off the dog or be removed. In addition to the tags, your vet can inject a small microchip between your Lab's shoulder blades. The chip has a number that will be registered to you and is a permanent way to identify your dog. The chip is read by a special scanner that most vets and rescue centres have. The chip number can be registered into a lost pet Internet database (several exist), and the finder can locate the pet's owner easily. Insertion of the chip is not painful and won't cause an allergic reaction.

Lead

Purchase both a 6-foot (1.8-m) lead and a 4-foot (1.2-m) lead, preferably the same

Puppies need a variety of toys to use when teething.

SENIOR DOG TIP

Older Rescued Labs

Labs from rescue centres and shelters usually aren't young puppies, but rather adults who lost their homes for a variety of reasons, not necessarily because the dogs did anything wrong. Older Labs who were socialised correctly tend to be mellower than some other breeds and will adjust to a new home if provided with the proper environment.

If you've adopted an older Lab, don't ask too much of him at first. Allow him to be successful in the home in small increments. If he has an toileting accident, simply take him outside and show him where to go. Also, give him a variety of toys and a bed placed in a quiet location.

learn to retrieve the lead before a walk, so make sure that the lead doesn't have any decorative items on it that can fall off and pose a choking hazard.

During the training process, you'll need a 25-foot (7.6 m) cotton long line that you'll use in the park or anywhere else you'll need to "reel in" your dog if he's not paying attention or has a tendency to run off. The long line is great for beginning to teach the *recall* command, as well as many other obedience commands.

Toys

Labs love chewing and retrieving toys, and puppies especially need a variety of toys to use for teething and to keep them occupied. Always buy toys sized appropriately for your Lab, because some can pose a choking hazard. Here's a list of toys that your Lab may appreciate:

- hard rubber "stuffable" toys
- soft squeaky toys
- rope/tugging toys
- rubber squeaky toys
- tennis balls
- treat-dispensing balls

material as your dog's collar—either nylon or leather. The 4-foot (1.2-m) lead is for training an adult Lab (to make sure you keep him close), and the 6-foot (1.8-m) lead is for fun walks (after lead training is complete) and hiking. Labs often like to hold the lead in their mouth while walking and will even

If you're a die-hard shopper, you can buy a lot of other goodies for your Lab, everything from designer dog beds to collars and clothes to show off his fashion sense. But Labs don't need these things to be happy. The basics are enough—along with plenty of tennis balls.

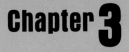

Chapter 3

Good Eating

As sporting gundogs, Labs require a high-quality diet to function like the athletes they are meant to be. Even the couch potato Lab needs a premium diet to prevent premature ageing, coat problems, and serious health issues.

Food Basics

A high-quality food is critical to a dog's health and well-being. Poor nutrition can cause health disorders as well as behaviour problems. Here is a rundown of the basic components of a high-quality canine diet.

Proteins

Proteins that dogs can use well come from animal sources, which is why it's important to serve a dog food that has a good-quality animal protein as its first ingredient and ideally as its second and third as well. Higher protein diets are indicated for puppies and very active dogs, but too much protein can cause kidney problems.

Fats

Fats are essential for coat, skin, kidney, and connective tissue health. Offer a low-fat diet only to an overweight dog. Relatively active dogs of a healthy weight should be allowed some fats. Fats also make food taste better, and they are often added at the end of the extrusion process in lesser-quality foods. You can add beneficial fats to your dog's diet by using

The right balance of fats in your Lab's diet will make his coat shiny.

omega-3 and -6 fatty acid supplements.

Carbohydrates

A balanced dog food is about 50 percent carbohydrates. In most dog foods, corn, soya, rice, potato, or wheat are the primary carbohydrates, and they are fine if they are from good-quality feed. Often, though, cheap feed—known as filler—is used, which adds little to no nutritional value to the food. You will know if your dog is reacting poorly to these fillers if he becomes bloated, gaseous, or develops allergies.

Supplements

Supplements are a controversial topic in canine nutrition. You will get different opinions from dog food manufacturers, vets, breeders, and dog owners—and each has valid points. Supplementing your dog with vitamins and minerals without knowing the balance of these items already in his food can cause health problems. Conversely, a dog who is on a poor diet or who is ill or very active may need extra nutrients to keep healthy. Before you supplement, speak with your vet and experts in the breed, and do some research of your own.

Your local pet store is likely stocked with dog supplements that all make various health claims. Some human-grade supplements, used conservatively, can enhance the diet without causing an imbalance, such as kelp and other green foods, flaxseed oil and fish oils, and some holistic supplemental blends made specifically for dogs. Beware of over-the-counter supplements in general, because you can never be quite sure that you're really getting the strength that the package claims.

27

Good Eating

Vitamins and Minerals

Both vitamins and minerals are essential for the body's functionality. High-quality dog foods contain sufficient vitamins and minerals, but some dogs may benefit from a supplement suggested by your vet.

Water

Your Lab should always have clean, fresh water available. An active Lab can become dehydrated easily, which can harm the kidneys and other organ systems. Often, during housetraining, some trainers recommend restricting your Lab's water intake shortly before bedtime until he can "hold it." This is fine as long as you remember to offer the puppy water often throughout the rest of the day, especially after he eats.

Reading Food Labels

When choosing a commercial food for your Lab, you have to understand a little bit about what the food labels claim so that you know what you're getting. Here's a short tutorial on what to look for on dog food labels.

Product Name

If the product name has the name of a food in it, like meat, chicken, or fish, it has to be 95 percent comprised of that type of food before water is added, and then it still must be made of 70 percent of the named food. For example, "Liver for Labs" dog food (a make-believe brand) must be 70 percent liver after the water was added. If it was called "Liver and Lamb for Labs," it must still be 70 percent liver/lamb after water was added, but it must contain more liver than lamb. The food mentioned in the name should be the first ingredient on the ingredient list.

"Dinner"

If the name of the product has "dinner" in it (or "formula," "nuggets," "entrée," or "platter"), for example "Liver

Dinner for Labs," the food must be at least 25 percent made of liver. Liver, in this case, will not be the first ingredient but probably the third, fourth, or fifth. If the name of the food is "Liver and Lamb Dinner for Labs," both food items must comprise 25 percent of the meal, but at least 3 percent of that must be lamb.

"With"

If a product claims that it has something "with" the main item, for example, "Liver and Lamb

When choosing a commercial food for your Lab, make sure that you check the food label for the list of ingredients.

Dinner for Labs With Bacon," the bacon part of the meal only has to equal 3 percent. If two items appear after the word "with," both have to be 3 percent of the meal separately.

Flavour

A food that says it is flavoured with something doesn't need to include a certain percentage of that flavour item in the meal. The company might add broth, by-products, whey, or chemicals to get that flavour.

Meat Source

The first ingredient on the list, ideally, should be a meat source, usually lamb, beef, chicken, or fish. Some dog foods include duck and venison as well. Chicken is a good first ingredient, especially chicken meal (because the water is already removed and more chicken

Treats

Treats are an integral part of training and account for a great deal of pleasure in a Lab's life. Some treats can be considered "junk food," like many of those you can find in your local supermarket. Many specialty pet stores, online retailers, and often some of the larger chain pet stores carry natural and low-calorie treats that are healthy for your dog and often add something important to his diet, like a supplement for joint or coat health.

ends up in the bag), and low-ash chicken is the best. Lamb is supposed to be less allergenic than other proteins. Beef meal will add more beef into the food than just plain "beef." Anything labelled "animal by-products" is suspect. These items may contain indigestible protein and even diseased animal parts and hide.

Fillers

Fillers can include rice hulls, corn, wheat, oatmeal, and even some appealing food items that are good for

Dry food is easy to feed and can help keep your Lab's teeth clean.

premium foods have better-quality fillers. Poor-quality foods might have fillers that came from sweeping the processing plant's floors or from grains that were too inferior to give livestock.

Preservatives

Beware of dog food that contains artificial preservatives. These can cause hair loss, cancer, allergies, kidney problems, and many other conditions. Artificial preservatives include ethoxyquin, butylated hydroxytoluene (BHT), and butylated hydroxyanisole (BHA). Natural preservatives include tocopherols (vitamin E) and ascorbic acid (vitamin C), which are much safer for your dog.

humans. Poor-quality fillers, like corn, aren't digested by the animal and shouldn't be in the food, or at least should be fifth or more down on the list of ingredients. Most dog foods have fillers, but

Commercial Foods

Commercial dog foods are easiest to feed. Simply open a bag or a can (or both), and put it in the bowl. It doesn't get easier than that. However, there are a lot of brands from which to choose, and you have to select carefully to give your dog the best nutrition possible. Making the wrong choice could cost your dog his health and rack up some serious veterinary bills.

In terms of choosing a commercially made food, think about this:

- The foremost requirement is that your dog likes it. It can be the best food in the world, but if your dog is going to fuss over it, there's no point in serving it.

- Make sure that the brand you choose has viable, usable nutrients—the more premium the food, the more viable the nutrients.

- Your dog should thrive on the food. If it is causing gas and intestinal problems, allergies (including itchiness and hair loss), or other health issues, change the food.

- Consider the "formula" of the food. There are formulas for puppies, active dogs, less active dogs, and seniors.

Dry Food

Dry 'complete' dog food contains about 10 percent moisture. It is made from either extruded or baked nuggets—choose baked, because it loses far less nutrients in the heating process. Dry food is the dog food "standard" and comes in many different qualities and standards. It is easy to feed and can help keep your dog's teeth clean. Mix in some water and canned food to make a more palatable meal.

FAMILY-FRIENDLY TIP

Feeding Time

Feeding time is an exciting time for a Lab, so it's nice to get the kids in the household involved. Supervised children can help by mixing the food, but an adult should offer the food bowl, because an eager Lab could knock a child over in his rush to get to the goodies. Tell the child to leave the dog alone while he's eating and to pick up the dish only when the dog has finished. Don't allow a child to be the only person responsible for feeding the dog, or that chore might not get done regularly.

Semi-Moist Food

Semi-moist dog foods contain about 40 percent moisture and are good for those dogs who won't eat dry food or who have teeth problems. Many of the commercial versions are full of artificial ingredients and sugars, but premium versions come in organic and all-natural formulas. Semi-moist dog foods also make good between-meal snacks or treats.

Table Manners

Table manners are critical for a large dog like the Lab. First, you should be teaching your Lab that he has to sit before he gets anything good, most especially food or a treat. Before you give him his bowl of food, he should have to sit nicely and look up into your face. (See Chapter 6 for more details.) Also, always feed your Lab after you eat your meal—the leader of the pack should eat first. Although your Lab may behave like he's starving while he waits, he is programmed to accept this, and he'll be just fine. Finally, treat any bowl or food guarding as very serious and unacceptable. It's an old myth that dogs should growl when you approach them while they're eating. A well-socialised dog understands that the bowl and the food are yours and that you have the right to remove them at any time. A dog who growls or shows his teeth when you approach or touch him while he's eating needs some serious training and re-socialisation.

Canned Food

Canned dog food is about 75 percent moisture—basically, you are buying a can of water. By law, canned dog foods cannot be more than 78 percent water, but if they are labeled "stew" or "with gravy," they can be up to nearly 88 percent water.

Premium brands still have a lot of moisture, but the ingredients are better, so they have a lot of nutrition, too. As mentioned earlier, if your dog likes canned food, you can mix a little bit of it with the dry food to improve the taste. This is an option that many people choose if they're using commercially prepared foods.

Non-commercial Diets

Some people choose to cook or prepare meals for their Labs, and this is indeed a viable option, albeit a costly and time-consuming one. But a healthy dog is worth the time and effort.

Cooked and raw diets should never be fed with dry food, because these meals digest differently. Entire books and websites are dedicated to both of these types of diets, so consult the experts and your vet before embarking on a new diet plan for your Lab.

Home-Cooked Diet

Most dogs love a home-cooked diet. These foods are much more savoury than the dry and canned stuff (although most Labs won't have a problem eating those, either!). The

Feeding Schedule for Each Phase of Your Lab's Life

	Puppies: 2 to 6 months	Adolescents: 6 to 18 months	Active Adults: 18 months to 6+ years	Sedentary Adults: 3 to 7+ years	Veterans: 7+ years
Times per Day	2–3	2	2	1–2	1–2
Amount	See label	See label	See label	See label	See label
Best Food	Puppy formula (protein less than 25%)	Active formula	Adult formula	Adult or senior formula (protein less than 22%)	Senior formula

people who feed a cooked diet claim that their dogs have more energy, shed less, and are leaner, and these diets don't contain preservatives. The real issue is time and feasibility. If you have the time to research this diet and prepare the meals (you can cook once a week and freeze the food in portions), then you may be the right candidate for this diet. It includes mostly human-grade foods, like low-fat cuts of meat, de-boned chicken, fish, fruits and veggies, healthy grains, yogurt, and human-grade supplements.

Raw Diet

The raw diet consists of raw meats and other ingredients, and it can be made at home or bought commercially in pet shops. The homemade version, often called BARF (bones and raw food), includes the bones in raw meat and chicken. Meat alone can be a nutritional disaster for dogs, but meat and chicken with the bones offer more balance. Usually, the wings, backs, and necks of the chicken are used because they don't splinter, along with organ meats, eggs, some veggies, and apple cider vinegar.

Never feed your dog cooked bones, because they can splinter and cause punctures in the digestive tract.

Feeding Schedules

Most people recommend against "free feeding"—that is, setting out an unlimited amount of food and allowing a dog to have his fill. This isn't good for any dog, and although it might work for some breeds, the Lab isn't one of them. Most Labs will stuff themselves and become ill if allowed to have all the food they want. In fact, free feeding will wreak havoc on a Lab's digestion and general health.

Making sure your Lab gets enough exercise will help keep him at a healthy weight.

Instead of allowing your Lab to gorge himself, feed him twice a day—once in the morning and once in the evening. After you've had breakfast and then again after you've had dinner are good feeding times. Puppies may need three smaller meals a day. Discuss mealtime with your vet to find out what's best for your dog.

Some evidence shows that feeding a dog a very large meal all at once (usually dry food) and then allowing him to exercise can cause a deadly condition called bloat, in which gas builds up in the stomach and the dog is unable to pass it or belch. The addition of exercise on top of the large meal

doesn't have to occur in order for bloat to happen. In some cases, the stomach rotates and closes off both the oesophagus and small intestine. To prevent bloat, feed two smaller meals a day, perhaps even three very small meals to a working dog on particularly active days.

Obesity

Obesity is as much an epidemic in the canine world as it is in the human realm. A lot of people tend to feed their dogs with love in mind, not health. Who can blame them? Labs love to eat, and what's better than making your dog happy with some table food or treats? There's nothing wrong with between-meal snacks, but a little goes a long way, especially with Labs. Labs tend to become overweight easily because they are built to be very active and hunt, but the average home isn't able to give them as much exercise as they need. Just as you might cut back on calories when you're not being as active, your dog has to do the same.

SENIOR DOG TIP

Counting Calories

As dogs get older, as with humans, they don't need quite as many calories to keep them going. If you notice your older dog getting chunky, switch him to a premium veteran-type dog food, or cut back a little on the food he's currently getting. Low-calorie treats, such as carrots, green beans, and freeze-dried chicken, are all better choices than fatty commercial treats. Older dogs also need more exercise. Even though your older Lab might not be moving so quickly anymore, that doesn't mean that he should just sit on the couch and vegetate.

Side Effects of Obesity

Overweight dogs can suffer from debilitating conditions, such as diabetes, joint problems, heart issues, and immune system dysfunction. Studies have shown that thinner dogs live dramatically longer and don't age as quickly. Don't think that an extra snack or two is going to make your dog's life better. On the contrary, those extra calories could eventually kill him.

How to Tell if Your Lab Is Obese

The "appropriate weight" for Labs is only a median range for males and females and does not take into account your individual dog's body type or whether he's a muscular working dog or a couch potato. Your vet will best be able to tell you what weight is appropriate for your individual dog. Don't let the scale itself determine whether or not you put your Lab on a diet and exercise programme. Instead, look closely at your dog in the following two ways:

1. First, feel his ribs. If you can feel them and the spaces between them and there's not a layer of fat over them, then he's probably a decent weight for his body type. If you can see his ribs, he's too thin.
2. Second, look at your Lab from above. He should have a waist. If he looks more like a sausage, he needs to lose a few pounds (kg).

What to Do if Your Lab Is Obese

If your dog does need to lose some weight, switch him to a low-calorie or veteran-type food and cut back on the amount of food that he gets. Limit table foods and snacks. He doesn't *need* them to survive. He does, however, need a vigorous game of fetch in the garden and a longer walk than usual. For most dogs, losing 1

Take the time to feed your Lab correctly and offer him enough exercise.

percent of their body weight per week is safe, but more can be dangerous, so don't put your dog on a crash diet. Like people, when dogs lose lean muscle mass because they aren't eating enough, they risk gaining that weight back in fat later.

Change the way you feed a hefty Lab. Instead of putting food in his dish, stuff his portions into a hard rubber toy and make him work for them. Scatter some of his food in the garden and have him hunt for his meal. Use his regular mealtime dry food as his treats rather than having additional treats in his diet.

Finally, implement an exercise programme for your overweight Lab or for any Lab who is not getting enough exercise. Start by making your daily walks just a couple of minutes longer until your dog is getting ten more minutes a day of exercise—that's over an hour more exercise a week, which can make quite a significant difference over time. This is not to mention how much exercise you'll be getting yourself. Healthy dog, healthy owner!

Take the time to feed your Lab correctly and offer him enough proper exercise. Try not to confuse food with love, as so many dog owners do. Your Lab will definitely beg for table scraps and more food in his bowl, but rather than giving in to his weaknesses, give him a good belly rub instead.

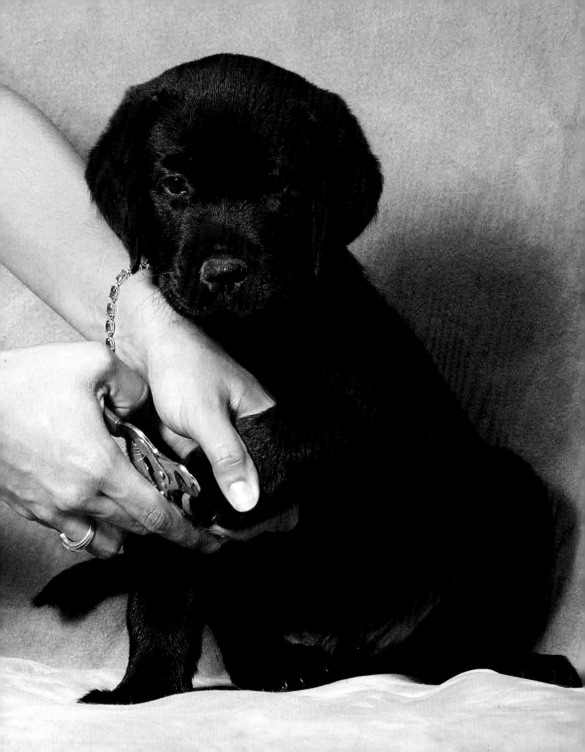

Chapter 4

Looking Good

The Lab's coat is considered "low maintenance" when compared to a breed that needs professional grooming, like the Poodle, but anyone who lives with a Lab will tell you that the "low" part of "low maintenance" is relative. Labs do shed quite a bit. In fact, some individuals "blow" their coat about twice a year, generally in the spring and autumn, and others shed all year long. In either case, you will need a good grooming regimen, along with a broom and a great vacuum cleaner.

The coat, skin, nails, ears, teeth, and eyes all need attention to be kept clean and healthy. Grooming is time consuming, but it can be a fantastic way for Labs and their owners to bond. Grooming can help prevent health issues as well and give the owner an opportunity to notice if any health problems are arising, such as dental issues, tumours, or eye problems. You can't help but to look closely at your dog while you're grooming, and if you do it regularly enough, any changes will be obvious.

Grooming Supplies

Here is a quick rundown of the grooming supplies you will need:
- curry brush (curry comb)
- dog conditioner (optional)
- dog shampoo
- doggy toothpaste and toothbrush
- nail clippers
- rake
- rubber hand brush or glove
- shedding blade
- slicker brush
- styptic powder or cornstarch
- washcloths
- wide-toothed comb

Getting Your Dog Used to Grooming

Dogs who are socialised to grooming early and in a positive manner tend to enjoy grooming. Start a grooming routine immediately after you bring your dog home. Be consistent, and treat grooming as a game. If grooming is fun for the owner, it will probably be fun for the dog, too.

Keep grooming sessions short, whether your Lab is a puppy or an adult dog who isn't used to being groomed. Reward your dog with treats for staying still and allowing his feet, muzzle, and ears to be touched. Don't force this kind of interaction. If your dog doesn't like having his feet touched, for example, try touching one foot for one second and then offer a treat. Then, touch the foot for two seconds and offer a treat, and so on. Eventually, you'll work up to holding a foot and inspecting the pads, in-between the pads, and the nails, but take it slowly and work up to it, especially with a puppy under 20 weeks of age, when any type of trauma may affect his perceptions for the rest of his life.

Brushing

Brushing your Lab is a good way to keep his coat and skin healthy. In fact, it removes dead hair and makes the coat more lustrous and healthy looking. It also stimulates the hair follicles and helps the natural oils from the dog's skin make the coat shiny and water resistant. Brushing also helps remove debris and dirt from the Lab's coat. Because Labradors shed, the hair might be particularly visible when it lands on your carpet, furniture, and clothing, depending on the colour of the dog. Thus, brushing is also a great way to limit the amount of hair that your Labrador leaves around the house.

In general, Labs only need to be brushed every few days, more frequently when the dog is blowing his coat. Loose and dead hair can be annoying or itchy for the Lab and can even hinder the coat's natural job of warming and cooling the dog. Brushing sounds like it would be a piece of cake, but you'll actually need a variety of tools to accomplish it properly. Here's a rundown of your weapons against hairballs under the bed:

- *Slicker brush:* This brush is usually flat and square, with needle-like bent pins sticking out from a rubber head. Use this brush first, going with the grain of the coat, to remove a lot of dead hair. Be gentle!

- *Wide-toothed comb:* After using the slicker, use the comb to remove the hair that the slicker left behind.

- *Rake:* It looks like it sounds! This comb is great for cutting down on shedding because its rubber nubs easily pull the dead hair out of the coat.

- *Shedding blade:* This loop of saw-toothed metal extends from a

Grooming as a Health Check

When you're grooming your Lab, you might discover health issues you would not have otherwise noticed, like ear mites, ticks, or tooth decay. In fact, grooming is more than just keeping your Lab looking good; it is also a way to help with the early detection of small problems that could turn into something more serious in the future.

brush handle and is good for removing debris and dead hair from the coat. Use this after the slicker and the comb but only when shedding is at its worst.

• *Curry brush (curry comb):* This short-bristled brush is good for an everyday once-over.

• *Rubber hand brush or glove:* This type of brush fits over your hand and is great for general brushing and even for bathing. Just lather the dog, put on the grooming glove, and wash away that dead hair.

Whatever combinations of brushes and combs you use, remember that brushing the Labrador involves more than just running the brush over the dog's back a few times. Brush the dog's sides, chest, neck, belly, legs, and

even the tail. Most dogs like to have the area under the chin brushed, as well as the top of the head. Avoid sensitive areas while brushing, like the nose and eyes. Remember to have some treats

If your dog loves being groomed, brush him for as long as he's enjoying himself.

Fleas and Other Pests

Warm, humid climates are a great breeding ground for fleas. Southern climes have the biggest flea problems, but summer in most places can cause a plague of fleas, especially for the Lab, a dog who loves the outdoors. Fleas cause itching, and dogs who are allergic to fleas can even lose hair, get sores, and acquire infections from scratching. You'll know if your dog has fleas when you see small black granules in his coat or bed. Add water to these granules, and if they dissolve and turn dark red, you'll know that your dog is infested—these granules are digested blood. Don't ignore fleas. They will not only make your dog uncomfortable and possibly ill, but they can infest your house and bite you as well.

Fleas can live anywhere on your dog, but they are especially fond of the eyes and around the base of the tail. If you find fleas and can catch them, kill them by pinching them between your fingernails. Treat the dog for a flea infestation with products that are indicated for safe use on dogs. The type of treatment depends on how severe the flea problem is; your vet or local groomer is a great resource for this issue. In general, you can get rid of fleas by using a topical pesticide treatment that you apply between the dog's shoulder blades. Your vet will be able to provide you with these products; the pet store version kills fleas that are currently on the dog but may not kill the eggs. Many of these treatments also repel ticks. Your vet can also provide you with tablets that the dog can take to interrupt the flea's life cycle. This medication does not kill fleas, but it does make the flea's eggs sterile.

Flea collars do work, but the Lab's coat is thick, which makes the collar less useful, and the collar must be kept dry. Flea powders, shampoos, and sprays kill fleas, but they only last a few days to a couple of weeks. Your groomer can "flea dip" your dog with a professional-strength insecticide that also kills the flea eggs, but you'll have to repeat this if the dog gets fleas again.

If the fleas have got into your carpet, sprinkle boric acid all over the carpet and work it in with a broom, wait a few minutes, and then vacuum. Do this a few times to make sure they're gone. Finally, you may have to use a pesticide "bomb" to kill all the fleas in your home.

handy just in case you make him uncomfortable during grooming. Treat liberally, and make brushing sessions as short as possible but long enough to get the job done. If you have a dog who loves his grooming time, then brush for as long as he's enjoying himself.

Ask your local grooming salon if they offer an "anti-shedding" bath. The groomer bathes the dog and strips all of the dead hair, and you usually won't have to worry about shedding for a couple of weeks. Never have your Lab shaved, thinking that you'll outwit the shedding. The dog will still shed anyway, but now he'll shed little prickly hairs instead of long soft ones. Also, the Lab's coat guards him against the weather and even keeps him cool in summer. If you remove the coat, you eliminate this natural protection.

Bath Time

A bath is really only necessary when your Lab smells bad, gets extremely dirty, or if he is shedding excessively. Bathing a Lab too often can dry out his skin, so give baths only when necessary. Fortunately, most Labs love water and won't put up too much of a fuss at bath time.

Your first concern when bathing a dog of this size is where you're going to do it. The family bath does work, but you're going to have Lab hair all over

Be sure to rinse all soap from your Lab before you dry him with a towel.

The Grooming Table

A professional pet groomer uses a grooming table to lift a dog up off the floor so that she does not have to bend over to work on the dog. The dog wears a special slip collar that is attached to a line on the grooming table to prevent him from jumping off. You don't need your own grooming table to work on your Lab. This breed is tall enough to work with on the floor, and it doesn't need extensive clipping.

the bathroom, from floor to ceiling. If you do use the bath, line the bathroom floor with towels so that the floor remains dry. Remove anything nearby that can be destroyed by water (like magazines or books). Purchase a shower hose attachment (you can get one at any pet store or online) so that washing is easy. If you don't have one, use a large plastic measuring jug with a handle to wet and rinse the dog.

On a hot summer day, it may be easier to wash your Lab outside. Make sure that the water from the hose isn't freezing cold, because that's going to be uncomfortable for the dog. The children in the household can put on their bathing suits and join in on the task (unless you're using a flea shampoo—then keep the kids out of the way). Hold the dog on a lead so that he doesn't run away with his coat full of soap. Use a cheap

plastic baby pool to put your Lab in at bath time. If your dog is balking at bath time, cut up a couple of hot dogs and toss them into the shallow water (before you've added any soap). Most Labs love to go fishing for hot dog slices and will jump right into the pool. Treat your dog as you bathe, and make the experience fun.

Wherever you decide to wash your Labrador, preparation is the key. Have all

The Expert Knows

Dewclaws

Dewclaws are known as a "vestigial toe" and are like the dog's "thumb," if he were to have one. The dewclaws don't touch the ground and serve no purpose. They are so named because they are said to touch the dew on the top of tall grasses. The Lab's dewclaws can be removed and still meet the requirements of the breed standard. In fact, you may want to have the dewclaws removed for safety reasons, because they can become painfully caught on something during hunting or playing. On the other hand, if they're small and out of the way, you might want to leave them alone. Removal of the dewclaw involves removal of both the nail and toe, but it's not a complicated procedure.

of your supplies ready before you bring your dog into the bathroom or garden. Use a shampoo that will not irritate his eyes, at least around his face. A simple baby shampoo will do, but many doggy shampoos on the market are made for sensitive areas as well. For the most part, use a shampoo meant for dogs, not humans. The pH balance is different in both types, and human soap can dry a dog's skin. Do not use bar soap or dish detergents on the Labrador's coat. If you like, you can also use a dog-specific conditioner, which will make the coat shiny, soft, and smell nice.

Start by wetting the dog thoroughly. The Lab's coat is water resistant, so rub the dog all over with your hands to soak in all the water. Wet his head, but tilt it back so that the water doesn't get into his eyes. Soap is less likely to run into his eyes if the area around them is dry. Avoid getting water into the ears as well. Lather the dog well, rubbing your hands with and against the coat in circles. If you're using a flea shampoo, you may have to let it sit a few minutes. Once you have thoroughly shampooed your Lab, make sure to rinse all the soap thoroughly off him before you begin to dry him with a towel.

If you live in a warm climate, the dog will dry himself while playing outside. Watch that your dog doesn't go straight from the bath to rolling in the dirt—this is one of the Lab's favourite tactics! If the weather is cold or you bathe the dog inside, towel dry him thoroughly, and allow him to shake off the remaining water. Then, blow-dry the dog on a low setting, making sure the air from the blow-dryer is not too hot. You can brush gently as you blow-dry, which will remove any remaining dead hair. Most breeders and groomers recommend

Children and Grooming

A young child can't thoroughly groom your Lab, but she can certainly help. Supervise all interaction between your child and your dog. You don't want the dog to associate grooming with something unpleasant. Teach the child how to be gentle when grooming, and to always brush with the grain of the coat. Children should not be allowed to clean your Lab's ears or eyes or trim his nails.

taking the time to blow-dry, especially if your dog sheds excessively.

Nail Care

Most dogs don't love having their nails cut, but it's a necessary part of the grooming process. Leaving the nails long can affect your Lab's gait, which will be uncomfortable for him. You'll know that it's time to cut the nails when you hear them clacking against hard floors.

If you're unsure how to properly cut your dog's nails, you can leave it up to your vet or grooming salon. If you want to try it yourself, you'll need the right tools. First, invest in a medium- to large-sized guillotine-style nail clipper that you can purchase at any pet shop. Don't try to use regular scissors or human nail clippers, because these can slip and injure the dog.

Your Lab's nail contains a blood supply called the *quick*. It's important to avoid the quick when you're cutting, or the nail will bleed and your dog will be wary of you coming near his paws again. In a dog with light-coloured nails, you can visibly see the quick; it's the pink line in the middle of the nail that extends nearly to the end. Cut just the tip of the nail. It is far more difficult to see the quick in a dog with dark-coloured nails. Be conservative about how much you cut. Ideally, cutting the

Cut just the tips of your Lab's nails, taking care to avoid the quick.

47

Looking Good

SENIOR DOG TIP

Grooming the Older Dog

When grooming an older dog, be aware of sore muscles and joints. Try to notice any aches or pains, and avoid those areas on the dog. Be careful not to move the dog's legs in an uncomfortable way while cutting nails. Brush the dog more gently than you would a younger dog. Most important, be sure to keep the dog warm when bathing him.

It is especially important to brush an older dog's teeth and have a vet examine his mouth regularly. Plaque on the teeth can affect the gums and lead to infections in the mouth and elsewhere in the body. A thorough teeth cleaning requires anaesthesia, which cannot be given to elderly animals or to those with certain health issues.

nails every few weeks will cause the quick to recede so that the nails can remain short.

If you do happen to cut into the quick, dip the nail into some styptic powder (you can get some at your local pet store) or into some flour or cornstarch to stop the bleeding.

Ear Care

The Labrador's ears also require routine cleaning. Ears are susceptible to mites and infection, so check them once a month to make sure that they are clean and healthy. The inside of the ears should be the same colour as the dog's skin; red blotches or other discolouration may indicate a problem. Infected ears might emit a strong, unpleasant odour. The dog might also become irritated and shake his head vigorously or scratch constantly at his ears. Ear infections require a vet's care.

Your vet or groomer will clean your dog's ears as a matter of routine, but you may want to clean them more often. To clean the ear, wrap a warm, damp cloth over your index finger and wipe down the inside flap of the ear. Next, moisten a cotton-wool ball with ear cleanser that you can purchase at a pet shop. Do not stick anything deeply into the ear; only clean the area visible to the eye. It is easy to injure the inside of the ear, so avoid the use of cotton swabs.

Eye Care

Remove discharge in the corners of the eyes by wiping them with a moist cloth. Keeping the eyes clean will help ward off infection and make the dog look much cleaner. This can be done as often as necessary, but if it seems that your Lab constantly has discharge in his eyes, it might indicate a problem, and the eye should be examined by a vet.

If you notice that your dog's brows or eyelashes are interfering with his eyes, you can trim those hairs to keep them out of the eye.

Dental Care

Like human teeth, a Labrador's teeth also require some care. Dog teeth are not as susceptible to cavities as human teeth are, so all that's required to maintain healthy dog teeth and gums is a cleaning once or twice a week to prevent plaque build-up.

Once plaque adheres to teeth and becomes tartar, only a thorough cleaning by a vet can remove it. This can be expensive for you and stressful to the dog, since it requires the dog to be put under anaesthesia. Thus, prevention is key.

It is much simpler to clean your Lab's teeth routinely at home. You can clean them with a piece of gauze, a thin washcloth, or a doggy toothbrush (a little rubber toothbrush that slides over your index finger). You can also buy special doggie toothpaste that tastes like liver, peanut butter, or chicken—however, never use human toothpaste

Keeping your Lab's eyes clean will help ward off infection.

on your dog because it gets frothy and is far less palatable. Also, your dog doesn't know to rinse and spit, and human toothpaste isn't meant to be swallowed. Put a little of the special toothpaste on the special toothbrush, and rub it over the front of your Lab's teeth. Unlike humans, the back sides of the teeth that face into the dog's mouth do not require much brushing, if any.

The movement of the tongue against the teeth can be enough to clean them.

Dry dog food and crunchy treats can scrape away plaque, too. Bones work in a similar way to keep teeth clean, as do hard plastic toys. These are simple things that you can do to help your Labrador avoid stressful, expensive visits to the vet for teeth cleaning.

Lab Attire and Accessories

The Lab has an "all-weather" coat and can stand cold climates and freezing water. Heat is somewhat less tolerable for the Lab, although his coat does help to insulate him against warm weather. A Lab who is in good physical condition should be able to deal with most types of weather with ease. Be careful, however, when you exercise your dog in hot weather, because Labs can get heatstroke if they get too warm or if they are not properly hydrated.

Some people help their Labrador brave the elements with sweaters, rain coats, or booties. Although your dog may appreciate some help with staying dry, these fashion accessories are not usually necessary. If you're inclined to dress up your Lab, go right ahead, but be aware that he might be the only Lab on the block in a tutu.

Grooming your Lab isn't optional—it's part of his daily care. Of course, he doesn't need extreme measures to keep him clean and his skin healthy, but he does need a little bit of consideration. Most Labs are content to roll in stinky-smelling stuff and then get into your bed at night and shed all over, so a lot of the grooming you'll do isn't just for him—it's for you.

Looking Good

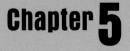

Feeling Good

Just as a person needs a yearly check-up, so does your dog. Not only are there vaccinations to consider, but a yearly visit allows your vet to monitor your dog's weight, dental health, and overall fitness. The vet can also detect parasites, tumours, or other health issues. Finally, if your dog goes to a veterinary surgery regularly, the vet is more likely to be able to treat your dog well during an emergency, not only because the vet will know the dog, but because the dog will also be used to being in the surgery and seeing the vet.

Finding a Vet

Finding an experienced vet with a good bedside manner is one of the most important things you can do to ensure your pet's health. Your vet is a person with whom you will have a relationship for the life of your Lab, hopefully well over ten years, so choose someone you like and who you feel listens to you and respects your dog.

It is actually much more difficult to become a vet than it is to become a medical doctor. Fewer veterinary schools exist, and they are very competitive. Vets also have to take continuing education courses throughout their lives to keep up with the latest information. Many vets specialise in aspects of illness just like other doctors—orthopaedics, oncology, radiology, pharmacology, and many other disciplines.

Get Recommendations

Instead of finding your vet in the phone book, ask your neighbours about their vet and find out if they're happy with the way the practice treats them and their dog. Dog sitters, people who work at rescue centres, breeders, and dog groomers can also give helpful suggestions.

Finding a good vet is one of the most important things you can do for your Lab.

Consider Proximity and Cost

The first two considerations for most dog owners are the location of the vet and the expense involved with treatment. It is important to have a vet close by in case of emergency. However, a vet whom you and your dog really love could be just a few minutes farther down the road. Proximity shouldn't be your only criterion. In terms of expense, everybody wants to get the most for their money. Nevertheless, the least expensive clinic might not provide the best treatment for your dog. You can find someone who will not leave you bankrupt and who will offer your dog the best possible care. Call and ask potential vets what a regular visit costs and how much yearly vaccinations are. These figures should give you a good idea of the differences in fee scales among the practices in your area.

Schedule an Impromptu Visit

After you create a list of practices to check out, schedule an impromptu visit for each, but go without your dog. Make sure the place looks and smells clean. Ask to go on a tour. This may seem overly involved, but there is really no other way to get to know the facility. Look at the kennels where the animals are kept for overnight stays, and find out if dogs and cats are separated. If your Lab has to stay overnight after surgery, will someone be there with him throughout the

FAMILY-FRIENDLY TIP

Visiting the Vet

The veterinary surgery might be a scary place for a child who doesn't understand what goes on there and whether or not the vet is going to hurt her best canine friend. After all, no one likes going to the doctor.

To reduce your child's fear, speak with her before the visit to inform her about what to expect during the examination. Stress that the vet is only trying to keep the dog healthy and that a vaccination only pinches for a second. Children also need to understand that they should be calm and give all the animals at the vet's surgery their space. In general, children should know not to pet unfamiliar dogs without asking the owner, but this is especially true of dogs at a veterinary surgery. Dogs under stress are more likely to behave aggressively.

night? Find out what the facility's hours are, if it is open 24 hours, and if it takes emergencies. Ask if the facility has a specialty, like cardiology or animal behaviour. What kinds of procedures does it perform in-house, and which ones require the consultation of outside sources? Find

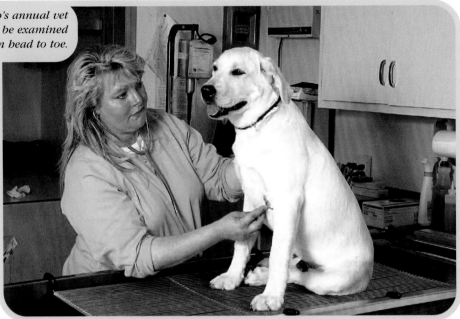

Labrador Retrievers

out how many vets work there and if you'll be able to choose which one your dog sees when you make an appointment. Consider the rest of the staff, too. Veterinary nurses are the people who provide most of the care for animals when they're recovering from surgery or staying overnight in the hospital. Veterinary nurses may also perform small procedures. If you like the vet but don't like the nurses, you may be better off elsewhere.

Make an Appointment for an Initial Consultation

Once you select a vet, make an appointment for an initial consultation. This way, you can observe the way that the vet and your dog interact. During this initial consultation, the vet will ask where you got your dog, how long you have had your dog, his age, and some other basic questions about his history. The vet will probably discuss the dog's breed and her thoughts on having the dog neutered. The vet should check the dog's eyes, ears, teeth, skin, and belly button, if he is still a puppy. The vet should also check your dog's abdomen, joints, and genitals for abnormalities.

It is also possible to have an initial consultation without engaging in any actual medical care if you really just want to make sure that you and your dog will like the vet. Watch how the vet behaves with the dog. Does she seem compassionate? Does she engage you in stories about Labs or tell you some history of Labs in her care? What's your general "vibe" about the vet and the surgery?

Find out if the practice operates an appointment service, or if there are times when you can come in if a problem crops up unexpectedly. In the UK, vets must offer 24-hour emergency cover, so find out how the practice provides this service.

A lot of vets do house calls, and some even have rolling hospitals, which are RVs outfitted with veterinary equipment sophisticated enough to deal with common surgeries. If getting your dog to the vet is a hassle, you may be able to have the vet come to you.

The Annual Vet Visit

Hopefully, if everything goes well, the only time your Lab will need to see the vet is during his annual visit, which should occur at about the same time each year. Most veterinary surgeries will send you a postcard to remind you to make an appointment. At this yearly visit, the vet will look your dog over from head to toe, checking for any abnormalities, as in the initial visit. A stool sample may be analysed to check for worms, and vaccines are given if needed. Certain vaccines are viable for different amounts of time, ranging from one to three years, so not every vaccine is necessary every year.

Neutering Your Labrador Retriever

If you're not going to breed your dog (a task best left up to professional breeders anyway), you should neuter your Lab as soon as your vet recommends, usually when the dog is six months to a year old. The spaying of female dogs involves removing all of their sex organs, whereas castrating for male dogs is defined by the removal of the testicles. For both males and females, "getting fixed" involves anaesthesia. For males, recovery happens quickly, but for females, the healing process can be longer and more involved.

Neutering male dogs tends to make them less aggressive and territorial,

Pet Insurance

Pet insurance is a phenomenon that has taken off during the past few years. Just like health insurance for humans, pet insurance helps cover the cost of health care. Some policies only cover accidents and illness, and others cover everything from routine visits and preventive care to yearly dental cleaning. Also, like human policies, the excess varies from policy to policy. Do your homework and read several policies thoroughly to ensure that the policy you choose is the type you need.

Vaccines can ward off a variety of illnesses.

and it decreases the dog's chance of getting prostate cancer. For owners of female dogs, oestrus can be an inconvenience, occurring twice a year for one or two weeks. The dog may become irritable at this time. She may whimper constantly, and she will attract male dogs from far and wide with her scent. Also, dogs who are not neutered are more likely to run away or fight with other dogs as they search and compete for a mate. Perhaps the best reason for having your Lab neutered is to prevent the birth of unwanted puppies. Rescue centres are already overflowing with great dogs who can't find homes.

Vaccinations

Vaccines are given as early as six weeks of age, and they will continue to be a part of your Lab's life every year. To be vaccinated, puppies should be weaned from their mothers, because breast milk contains natural antibodies that can interfere with vaccines. Puppies must also be healthy before receiving vaccines, which is why a physical check-up always precedes vaccinations and booster shots.

The specific vaccinations offered will depend on your vet's advice and where you live. For example, all dogs living in the US must be vaccinated against rabies, but this would not apply in the UK. Rabies is a viral infection that attacks the nervous system, causing irrational behaviour, foaming at the mouth, and eventually death. It can be spread to any mammal, including humans, through a bite by an infected animal.

Other diseases that dogs are generally vaccinated against include bordetella (kennel cough), canine coronavirus, distemper, hepatitis, leptospirosis, Lyme disease, parainfluenza, and parvovirus.

- *Bordetella ("kennel cough")* is characterised by a raspy, nagging cough; it is spread through contact with infected dogs. It is generally not fatal.
- *Canine coronavirus* is a viral infection that affects the intestinal tract.
- *Distemper* is a disease that can

cause vomiting, diarrhoea, pneumonia, neurological problems; it can be fatal.

- *Hepatitis* is a viral disease that affects the lungs, live, kidneys, and spleen.
- *Leptospirosis* affects the liver and kidneys; it can be spread to humans through a dog's urine.
- *Lyme disease*, which can affect those dogs who spend a great deal of time in the woods or outdoors, is spread through tick bites and can cause lameness, fever, and joint and muscle damage.
- *Parainfluenza* is an infection of the upper respiratory system, and like human influenza, it is very contagious.

One single vaccine can ward off all these illnesses and eliminate a serious health risk for you, your family, your other dogs, and all the other animals they might come into contact with on a regular basis.

Following vaccination, many dogs will be sore or sluggish for a couple of days. Extreme reactions aren't common, but they do occur. A severe reaction can include hives or vomiting. In rare cases, some dogs get tumours from vaccines. If you notice a reaction after any vaccines, make your vet aware of the situation as soon as possible. In the case of hives, a simple antihistamine is generally enough to alleviate the reaction.

Parasites

Parasites are animals that live on or inside your dog and can cause health problems ranging from minor and irritating to deadly.

External Parasites

External parasites are generally insects that feed on a dog's blood, causing him irritation and skin problems.

Fleas

As mentioned in Chapter 4, the flea is the most common parasite that dogs experience. Flea bites itch and can cause severe allergic reactions in some dogs. They also bite humans and can infest an entire house. Once they are established, it's very difficult to get rid of them. Because they have a four-stage life cycle (eggs, larvae, pupae, and biting adults), they are very resistant to extermination and preventive methods.

You will know you have fleas if you see "flea dirt" on your dog or in his bed. The little granules that fleas leave behind are their faeces, and these are actually mostly dried blood. Take some of the granules and put them on a white napkin or paper plate and put a few drops of water on it—if it turns red, you have fleas.

Preventing fleas is your first defense. Your vet can prescribe a topical application that is spread between the dog's shoulder blades. This pesticide controls both adult fleas and their eggs. Similar products control one or the other. You can also use a safe insecticide in your home or in outdoor areas to prevent a flea infestation if you live in a warm climate. A pill is also available that your dog can take to sterilise any fleas that bite him, which eventually leads to flea death.

If your dog already has fleas, shampoo him with a product specifically for killing fleas, and use a flea dip (which you pour over and leave on the dog) if the infestation is particularly nasty. Sprinkle borax into your carpet, rub it in with a broom, and then vacuum it up after a few hours.

Also sprinkle it under your bed and mattress. You can also "bomb" the house with a fumigator made especially to get rid of fleas. Plenty of flea products are on the market, and many of them work very well when used together. There are many different types of flea, so ask your local vet about the best methods of killing the fleas in your area.

Mites

Two types of mites typically are found on dogs: *sarcoptic mites* and *demodex mites.* Both of these mites cause a skin condition called *mange.* The sarcoptic mites, also called *scabies,* are highly contagious among dogs and can pass to humans as well. This type of mange is tricky to diagnose, so it may be mistaken for other skin conditions as it continues to get worse. Symptoms include intense itching, hair loss, crusty bumps on the skin (which can have a rotting odour), and lesions at the edge of the ears. If you suspect scabies, rub the inner edge of your dog's ear with your finger, and watch to see

Feeling Good

if he pedals the leg on the same side in a scratching motion (a reflexive reaction). If so, he probably has the condition and will need treatment, which includes several insecticidal dips (performed by your vet) and perhaps an injection.

The demodex mite causes the same symptoms as the sarcoptic mite but less intensely. It is diagnosed by looking at a skin scraping under a microscope and is also treated with several insecticidal dips. It can be passed to humans, but that is very rare.

Both of these mites occur on dogs kept in unclean conditions, as well as those having a suppressed immune system, such as a dog who isn't getting proper nutrition. However, dogs kept

clean and healthy can still get demodex as puppies from their mother, even if the mother has never shown symptoms of mange.

Ticks

Labradors love to play outside, which can leave them vulnerable to ticks. Unlike fleas, ticks aren't terribly obvious, and they often go unnoticed. You will most likely discover ticks while petting or brushing your dog, and they will feel like nothing more than a bump on the skin before you investigate further.

If you spot a tick, do not attempt to burn it or put anything on it, like petroleum jelly, two old-fashioned remedies. The best way to remove a

tick is by taking a pair of tweezers, gripping the tick as close to the skin as possible, and pulling it slowly out of the skin. Do not twist or jerk the tick out. If you grip the tick too far back, the back end of the tick will come off, leaving the mouthparts behind. If this happens, the mouthparts will be harder to see and grip, but they must be removed because they can cause infection. If you can't get the tick's head out, take your dog to the vet. Clean your Lab's wound with rubbing alcohol or another disinfectant to minimise the chance of infection.

In the US, the deer tick spreads Lyme disease. This is rare in the UK, but its incidence is increasing.

Internal Parasites

Internal parasites are less easy to see than external parasites, but they are no less a nuisance. Do not disregard the symptoms of internal parasites—they can be deadly.

Roundworms

Roundworms infest the small intestine and interfere with digestion. They can give the dog a shabby, malnourished another animal that has the parasite. The worms show up in faeces and vomit, and your vet can test a faecal sample to detect them as well. Treatment with a common dewormer is effective, but it must be repeated after two weeks to kill the larvae that matured after the treatment.

Heartworms

Heartworms are rarely a problem in the UK. There parasites are transmitted through mosquitoes carrying infected blood. The *microfilaria*, the larval form of the heartworms, enter the dog's body and go to the heart and arteries, where they grow and reproduce. Heartworms can grow to be 1 foot (0.3 m) long and can live up to seven years. Symptoms may not occur for up to a year. These may begin as a cough, laboured breathing, and weight loss and then appear later as kidney and liver damage. The dog seems lethargic and tired in general and may also lose consciousness in later stages—the prognosis for an infected dog is grim. If heartworms go untreated, the dog eventually dies. A blood test can diagnose the presence of heartworms

A balanced diet and plenty of exercise will have a positive effect on your Lab's physical condition.

appearance and swollen belly and can cause anaemia and even pneumonia as the larvae move through the respiratory system. They are transmitted from mother to puppy during gestation or nursing or by ingesting the eggs, often from eating

SENIOR DOG TIP

The Ageing Lab

Labradors are considered senior citizens when they are about eight years old, although the ageing process varies from dog to dog. When the Lab does start to age, some problems he may experience include hearing loss, change in coat, joint stiffness, arthritis, and decreased ability to fight off disease. Regular veterinary visits, a veteran diet, and help manoevring (for example, in and out of the car) will all help the older Lab live comfortably into his golden years.

but not until the worms have been in the dog at least six to seven months, after they mature. X-rays can confirm diagnosis. An infected dog is treated with medications and possibly surgery.

Fortunately, you can get monthly heartworm preventives from your vet, if required. Your dog will not start these treatments until he has been deemed negative for heartworms.

Hookworms

Hookworms attach to the dog's intestines and feed on his blood, causing anaemia and digestive disorders, such as vomiting and diarrhoea. A stool sample analysed by a vet demonstrates the presence of hookworms, which are treated using one of many common deworming treatments. The monthly heartworm preventative also prevents hookworms.

Ringworm

Ringworm isn't actually a worm, it's a fungus that grows on the skin and causes patches of hair loss and itching. It is also transmissible to humans. Diagnosis is usually done visually or by looking at the skin using a black light. A culture of the affected area can also help to diagnose ringworm. Treatment includes fungicidal shampoos, creams, and in some cases, oral medication.

Whipworms

Whipworms infest the dog's large intestine and cecum (appendix). A dog gets whipworms by eating their eggs, which are found in soil. Dogs who eat soil or walk in soil and lick their feet are at risk. Whipworms create digestive disorders, including diarrhoea that comes and goes. Eventually, the damage caused by these worms can cause a bacterial infection. Treatment is effective using a common dewormer. Whipworms can be avoided with a heartworm preventative.

Breed-Specific Illnesses

Even with yearly care and the proper preventives, Labradors might still experience medical problems. Labs as a breed are most prone to dwarfism, hip dysplasia, and progressive retinal atrophy (PRA). These ailments are not preventable, because they are largely genetic disorders, but knowing the lineage of your dog will help you to gauge the likelihood of any of these ailments becoming a problem in the future. Responsible breeders try to breed out these genetic disorders in their breed lines.

Dwarfism

Dwarfism in Labradors is characterised by short, bowed legs and a large head. Dogs suffering from this disease feature elbows that stick out and hind legs that are straighter than normal. Dogs with dwarfism are more likely to have joint problems, eye problems, and experience hip dysplasia. Treatment includes growth hormones and thyroid medication.

Your vet will be able to detect any eye abnormalities in your Lab.

Hip Dysplasia

Hip dysplasia is found to some degree in every breed of dog that grows to be over 35 pounds (15.9 kg). The ligaments of the hip, which should hold the joint tightly in place, become loose and allow the various parts of the leg to wobble and collide with one another, slowly causing damage to the joint and eventually resulting in pain, decreased mobility, and arthritis. Hip dysplasia is genetic, but even two healthy parents can produce a puppy who has hip dysplasia. A dog with severe hip dysplasia should not be bred from.

65

Feeling Good

Food allergies are common in Labs.

When a dog is two years old, he can be tested for hip dysplasia through an X-ray. The X-ray is then scored in a joint scheme run by the Kennel Club and the British Veterinary Association. Overall, fewer Labradors have problems with hip dysplasia today than they did just 20 years ago, a positive sign for the breed.

Treatment of hip dysplasia includes pain medication, anti-inflammatory medication, and rest. Your vet also can discuss several surgeries with you so that you are able to choose the right one for your dog's particular condition.

PRA and CPRA

Labradors are also prone to progressive retinal atrophy (PRA) and central progressive retinal atrophy (CPRA). Both involve the light receptors in the retina, causing reduced vision, blind spots, and blindness. Sometimes the light receptors are destroyed and sometimes the retina folds. In extreme cases, a dog might experience retinal separation, cataracts, or enlarged eyes. In the case of PRA, the first sign is night blindness. In CPRA, vision is affected but the dog may not become blind. Dogs with these conditions should not be bred from.

Puppies who have this disorder

generally exhibit symptoms soon after birth, and a vet should be easily able to detect that something is wrong. No treatment exists, as of this writing, but retinal transplants may be possible in the future.

General Illnesses

You must watch for other diseases and ailments that affect all types of dogs. These include allergies, cancers, Cushing's disease, diabetes, ear infections, and eye infections.

Allergies

Dogs can have allergies, just like humans. Food allergies are common, as are allergies to fleas, dust mites, and mould. The main symptom of allergies is itchiness and the resulting hair loss and open sores caused by scratching. Also, look for licking and chewing of the legs and paws. If you suspect that your dog has allergies, take him to the vet, because itching can present in a number of other illnesses.

Your vet can do skin testing to try to determine the cause of allergies. Your vet can also give your dog medication that will make him more comfortable during allergic periods. This may include topical ointments, steroid shots, and antihistamines.

Cancer

Dogs can get cancer in any of their organs, just as humans do. Symptoms

First-Aid Kit

Your doggy first-aid kit should include the following:
• Antibacterial ointment
• Benadryl
• Canine anti-inflammatory
• Cloth tape
• Eye wash
• Gauze bandages
• Gauze sponges
• Hydrocortisone cream
• Hydrogen peroxide
• Pepto-Bismol
• Petroleum jelly
• Scissors
• Self-adhering bandages
• Splints

Have the dog's paperwork, regular medicines, a blanket, a thermometer, and a muzzle in the kit as well (in case your dog must be restrained). Take the kit on trips, and keep it in an accessible place while at home. Dogs are susceptible to many of the same traumas and small ailments as humans, such as heat exhaustion, cuts, and allergies, among others, and you can easily begin treatment for small traumas at home. For most injuries, however, stabilise the dog and get him to a vet as quickly as possible.

Regular preventive care will keep your Lab happy and healthy.

vary with the different kinds of cancer. Take your dog to the vet if you notice a growth, tumour, wheezing or coughing, or weight loss. Cancer in dogs is treated very similarly to cancer in humans. Some forms are easier to treat than others. To help prevent cancer in your dog, spay your female before her first heat cycle, which will protect her from cancers of the reproductive organs. Castrate your male dog, especially if his testes haven't descended. As with humans, keep your dog away from carcinogens, such as cigarette smoke. Limit his exposure to pesticides (including flea and tick preventives).

Cushing's Disease

Older dogs can also sometimes develop Cushing's disease, also called *hyperadrenocorticism*. This disease is characterised by a tumour either on the pituitary gland (in 85 percent of cases) or adrenal gland (in 15 percent of cases) that causes the gland to produce too much adrenocorticotropic hormone, in the case of the pituitary gland, or too much cortisol, in the case of the adrenal gland. This throws off the body's natural balance and manifests as an increase in appetite, panting, high blood pressure, changes in skin colour and texture, hair loss, thirstiness, more frequent urination, a bulging abdomen, and nervous system disorders. These symptoms can sometimes be confused for other problems, but treatment can begin once a diagnosis is made through a blood test. Left untreated, Cushing's disease can be fatal—the dog may succumb to heart failure, liver failure, or infections. Treatments include medications and surgery (if the Cushing's is due to a tumour).

Diabetes

Dogs can also get diabetes, especially if they are overweight—but the condition is not limited to overweight dogs. Diabetes is a result of a hormone imbalance, and it is characterised by excessive drinking and urination, as well as weight loss. If left untreated, the dog can have kidney problems and may develop cataracts. Dogs with diabetes require insulin injections to regulate their blood sugar. Some owners can regulate their dogs' blood sugar using a specialised diet and an exercise programme.

Ear Infections

Ear infections occur from the build-up of moisture or wax in the ear canal. Mites can also infect the ears. Usually, infected ears smell sort of sweet and rotten and have a yellow or brown sticky substance inside them. The dog scratches them and shakes his head. Labs who swim a lot are particularly prone to ear infections.

   If you suspect an ear infection, take your dog to the vet. Treatment usually consists of cleaning out the ear

every day with a special solution, antibiotics, and keeping the ear free of hair and moisture. Some over-the-counter remedies work well to prevent or clear up ear infections, such as putting a little vinegar inside the ear and then swabbing it out. Never, ever put a cotton bud into your dog's ear—only use cotton-wool balls and a finger, and be gentle.

Eye Infections

Eye infections can occur due to an injury to the eye, a foreign body or chemicals in the eye, dental problems, dehydration, or any disease that causes the eye to dry out. Symptoms can include red eyelids, watery eyes, and scratching of the eye. If you suspect a foreign body, chemicals, or an injury to the eye, flush it with saline solution

If you suspect your Lab is suffering from an ear infection, take him to your vet.

What Is a Holistic Vet?

A holistic vet deals with an animal's health by taking the whole body into account and considering how it works as a system, including emotional factors like stress and the animal's relationship with his owner. Holistic medicine is less invasive than traditional medicine and includes treatments that centre around herbal medicine, dietary needs, homeopathy, chiropractic, behaviour modification, augmentation therapy, and acupuncture, possibly in conjunction with traditional medicine. Holistic medicine tries to consider the entire pattern of an organism's health and the possibility of several factors contributing to illness, not just one disease or condition. Holistic vets can be found in much the same way as regular vets, by word of mouth or by recommendation. Or you can log onto the Vet Index website (www.vetindex.co.uk), which lists vets who practise complementary medicine.

dangerous, but they can be very powerful and cause side effects. Even if an alternative therapy is not the main source of treatment, it might help the dog feel more comfortable. Many vets are offering alternative treatments in their practices.

In particular, allergies and arthritis are often treated somewhat successfully using alternative treatments. Vitamins, chondroitin sulfate, glucosamine, and fatty acid supplements have all been reported to offer some relief to dogs with degenerative joint diseases. Fatty acids can help with skin and coat health, which in turn can help relieve allergies.

and see if that helps the symptoms. Take your dog to the vet as soon as possible.

Alternative Therapies

In addition to traditional medicine, alternative ways are available to deal with illness in a dog. These often are called "complimentary medicine." They can be used alone or in conjunction with traditional medicine, but alternative therapies should only be given by licensed professionals. Herbs and supplements might not seem

Acupuncture

Acupuncture is an ancient method of healing that involves very small needles stuck into specific points in the body to get the body's natural energy flowing. Dogs react very well to this treatment and find relief for a variety of ailments, from arthritis and lameness to sinusitis and circulatory problems and many more. It is worth asking your vet about a licensed veterinary acupuncturist in your area if your dog has a chronic disorder or is experiencing acute pain. Acupuncture can be used as a primary therapy, although it is often used in conjunction with more traditional Western medicine.

Herbal Therapy

Herbal therapy is part of a holistic treatment plan that works to help the body heal itself by boosting the immune system. As with homeopathic treatments (mentioned below), countless herbal therapies can help with various symptoms and diseases. Consult with your vet before embarking on any herbal therapy programme.

Homeopathy

Homeopathy was founded in the early 1800s by a doctor who believed that the body could heal itself when stimulated by substances that caused symptoms similar to those of the disease. Books on homeopathic treatments for dogs detail what kinds of substances (found at most health food stores) should be given for any particular symptoms.

Health care is critical for the long life of a Labrador, an active dog who is bound to have aches and pains along his journey of life. Take care of him by educating yourself about canine health care, and make sure that he has a caring, qualified veterinary surgery whom he sees regularly.

Feeling Good

Herbal therapy works to help the body heal itself.

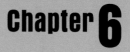

Chapter 6

Being Good

Training is not optional, especially for a high-energy, large dog like the Lab. Dogs don't train themselves to be well-behaved members of the household. They will behave however they desire to get what they need. In the case of a Lab, that means counter-surfing for goodies, scratching at the door to be let out, and jumping on guests for attention. All these undesired behaviours, and many others, can be changed with just a little training.

Positive Training

The most effective type of training uses positive reinforcement to condition desired behaviours into a dog. It's much easier to train a behaviour into a dog than it is to change a current behaviour. Using positive reinforcement, you reward a desired behaviour every time it occurs, but you ignore other behaviours. The dog soon understands that if he does something you want him to do, he'll get a treat, praise, or toy, but if he doesn't do the right thing, he won't get anything. This type of training allows a thinking breed like the Lab to work problems out on his own and to try different behaviours to give you what you want.

Clicker Training

Clicker training is a good example of a training method that uses positive reinforcement as its root. With clicker training, you use a small noisemaker (the clicker) to mark a desired behaviour. After the click and desired behaviour has occurred, you should dole out a reward—in the case of Labs, a soft, small, chewy treat should work, something that he can eat in one gulp without stopping to chew and interrupting training.

When you begin to clicker train, you first have to "prime" the clicker to show your dog that treats occur after the click. This conditions the dog to associate the click with the treat. Thus, you click and then treat, and click and then treat until your dog looks up expectantly at you when you click. At this point, you know that he has made the connection. You should prime the clicker a few times before every training session.

When you train certain behaviours, like the *sit*, you use the clicker to reward the moment when the dog engages in the behaviour, and then you treat. The click tells the dog that what he has done is right, and he is more likely to do it again because he got positively reinforced for it. Once he starts offering the *sit* behaviour on his own, you can add the verbal

The Expert Knows

Finding a Trainer

Most first-time dog owners should consult a professional trainer or take a group class to learn the basics. The Kennel Club has details of all training clubs in the country, or you can find a trainer by personal recommendation, such as asking your vet or enquiring at a local rescue centre. You can look in the phonebook or online, too, and ask the trainers you find there to give you references that you can call. Also, ask what training methods the trainer uses and if she has worked with Labs before.

command to sit. Now he will come to understand that the motion of him putting his rump onto the ground is connected to the word "sit," and every time he's in the process of sitting he'll get a click, and once the click happens he'll get a treat.

This kind of training is quick and easy once you get the hang of it. It's important to be quick with the clicker and to only click when the behaviour is in

process, not when it's over. For example, click as the dog is sitting, not when he's getting up from the *sit*, or else you'll be reinforcing him getting up from the *sit*, not the action of sitting itself. Don't add the verbal cue until the dog understands the behaviour for which he's being clicked.

You don't have to use a clicker to do this kind of training. Choose a word that you like— "yes," for example—and use that instead of the click sound. The clicker is good, however, because it always sounds the same; it is loud and distinct, and it doesn't have any intonation that can confuse the dog.

The most effective type of training uses positive reinforcement.

Treats

Be generous with treats. Don't skimp on the reward or else your dog will have little reason to keep paying attention. Some Labs learn well with treats and a ball toss for especially good behaviour. Find out what your dog likes best, and use that as your reward.

Length of Training Sessions

Keep training sessions short, especially for puppies. Two to five minutes a few times a day should do for a young dog, and ten minutes should be fine for an older dog.

Socialisation

Socialisation is simply about introducing a puppy to

Training Treats

Training treats should be bite-sized and very soft so that the dog can swallow each one down in one gulp. If the treat is too large or crunchy, he will have to stop to chew it, which interrupts the training session. Some companies now make soft training morsels, or you can use finely chopped, bite-sized hot dogs or small bits of cheese. Ideally, the treats should be fragrant so that the dog will be extra eager for them. Labs have a "will work for food" attitude, so they are more apt to pay attention to training sessions if you have something edible that they really want.

everything he might run into as an adult dog—traffic, balloons, playground equipment, vacuum cleaners, fireworks, grooming, and so on.

The period of real socialisation occurs when a puppy is about 4 to 20 weeks old. After that, socialisation is much more difficult, although not impossible. During the puppy socialisation period, the puppy must be introduced to as many new people, animals, objects, surfaces, touches, and situations as possible. At this stage, the puppy is eager to accept new things with wide-eyed interest. After this time, new people, animals, and situations may be viewed with suspicion or fear.

Socialising Your Puppy to People, Places, and Things

Every new object and situation should be made fun and pleasant for the puppy. If something scares him during the socialisation period, he may regard it with fear for the rest of his life. For example, if he's traumatized at the grooming salon when he's a puppy, he may never overcome his fear of going there. So, while he's still learning about the world, keep his life as pleasant as possible and show him that people of all sizes, shapes, and colours are all fun to meet. Give people treats and have them feed and pet your puppy. Have him meet lots of other dogs of all breeds and sizes, and only intervene in playtime if it gets genuinely rough and your puppy is cowering

Socialising your Lab puppy is critical to his emotional development.

in fear. He should also meet cats, birds, and other small pets, with the proper supervision, of course.

Socialising Your Puppy to Children

Most critically, dogs should be well socialised to children. Children can be intimidating to a puppy or dog who isn't used to how they move and behave. It's just as important, if not more so, to teach children how to behave around dogs. It's not really your own children you have to worry about, though, but kids your dog doesn't know who might rush up to him, tease him, or pull his ears and tail.

Start socialising your dog to accept touch by touching him on the places that a child is most likely to bother— the tail, ears, paws, and muzzle. After you touch each spot, offer a small, moist treat. When he's used to those touches, touch each area again, lingering a moment on the touch before you treat. Next, gently tug the ears and the tail, treating after each touch. Hold the muzzle closed for a moment, and then treat. Lift each of the paws and treat after each one. Keep doing these exercises until you can closely inspect each paw, look at the dog's teeth, hold the muzzle shut for five seconds, look inside the ears, and lift the tail, all without the dog caring one bit about what you're doing.

Crate Training

The crate isn't punishment or a place to give your dog a "time-out" when he's in the way. The crate is simply used as a space for your dog to rest when you can't supervise him. The crate prevents him from having accidents in the house and from destroying anything when you're not right there to keep an eye on him. Remember

Being Good

Dog Body Language

Doggy body language is how dogs communicate, and your dog will be looking at you for clues on how to behave. Here are a few hints on how to most effectively train your dog while taking body language into account:

1. Don't stoop or kneel when training. Making yourself smaller or putting yourself on the dog's level might show him that you're being submissive.
2. If your dog is doing something that you don't like, try a little growl and a stare; that's how the leader of the pack would warn an underling. Don't stare too hard, however, because that can be intimidating.
3. Don't stare at a fearful dog, but instead look indirectly at him with your body turned away.
4. Yawning can be a sign of fear or nervousness in dogs. If you have a fearful dog, yawn and sigh to put him at ease.
5. Mounting is one way that dogs show dominance. If your dog is mounting you or other family members, put him back on the floor so that he has all four feet touching the ground, and then place one hand on his shoulders and one on his back and keep them firmly placed there for a few moments. Don't be forceful; just show him that you're the alpha in the house and that you can touch him like this, not the other way around.

that a dog can only stay in the crate about as long as he can "hold it." A puppy can only spend a couple of hours in the crate, perhaps less, and an adult dog should not spend more than four hours in the crate at once.

Positive reinforcement training works well for crate training. (See Chapter 2 for instructions on how to properly choose the right kind of crate.) Once you have the crate and it's in the right spot, take off the door to the crate, and put it aside. Place a comfy mat or bed inside the crate. Lure your puppy or dog into the crate using a treat. Once he's inside and still facing the back of the crate, click and treat (or say, "Yes!" and treat). Allow him to come out, but be calm and don't interact with him. Lure him inside again and repeat. Praise him highly! Remember to praise him when he's inside the crate during training sessions, but be indifferent when he's outside of it.

If your puppy is reluctant to go inside, click and treat him for stepping just one paw on the edge of the crate, and once he has got the idea, raise the criteria of what you're looking for, and wait until he has two paws at the edge of the crate. Work slowly, and don't ask for too much too soon.

When your puppy has the hang of this and starts wandering inside the crate looking for the treat, reward him for going inside and turning around. Put the door back onto the crate and repeat the steps from the beginning. Once he's comfortable in the crate, close the door for one second when he's inside, click and treat, and then open it. Repeat until you can close it for a few seconds without him becoming upset that he's confined.

Your next step is to have him inside the crate with the door closed as you get up and take a step away from it. If he's calm, come right back, click and treat, and let him out. Repeat until you can walk all the way across the room while he's calm. One trick is to give him something really good to chew while he's in the crate, like a rubber toy stuffed with fragrant foods. This way, he's distracted and having a good time. This kind of training is geared toward making learning fun. If your dog is upset or not doing well, just quit the training session for the day, but not before you can get one calm second from him when he's in the crate. End each session on a positive note.

If you do this kind of training gradually, you will work up to being able to leave the room, then leave the house, all while your dog is content inside the crate. If you simply shove your dog inside and lock the door and leave, he's not going to understand that you are coming back, and he may panic, making the crate a place to fear.

Housetraining

Housetraining should start the minute you bring your puppy home. You will need to watch for signs that your dog needs to relieve himself and anticipate that moment. Once you have an idea of your

The crate is a safe place for your Lab to rest when you are unable to supervise him.

FAMILY-FRIENDLY TIP

Children and Training

Children are great at helping to teach the *come* command. Start a game with as many children as you'd like, putting them in opposite points of the garden or park (with the long line on the dog), and give them treats. Have them take turns calling the dog by name and using the *come* command and then treating the dog when he responds. Be careful about allowing children to teach any other commands, however, because a few slip-ups can set training back.

puppy's toileting schedule, you can pick him up and walk him outdoors to the area where you want him to go. Usually, puppies need to toilet in the morning, just after meals, after waking up from a nap, and before bed.

When your puppy relieves himself outside, praise him and offer him treats. If you catch him in the act of relieving himself inside, pick him up immediately and take him to the spot you'd like him to use. Don't make a big fuss about it. If you notice that he has relieved himself inside after the fact, there's nothing you can do. Don't punish the dog or rub his nose in it.

These tactics don't teach anything and actually teach your dog that relieving himself is wrong and that he should fear you. Instead, reward your dog when he properly relieves himself outside, and he will most likely continue to toilet there.

Basic Commands

Any well-behaved Lab should know a handful of behaviours to get along in a world ruled by humans. The following are the five main commands that you should begin teaching as soon as your puppy is ready. You will use the word "okay" to release your dog from any command you give him.

Come (Recall)

The first command, or cue, that you will teach your dog is the *come*. Use the word "come" and your dog's name to get him to come to you. There are only two occasions where you'll use your dog's name—to call him to you or to get his attention. In both cases, use his name positively. Never use his name to scold him or to call him to you to reprimand him. What's the point of coming to you if you're going to be unpleasant? Every time you call the dog, he should expect to get something good, either a treat, a game, or a head scratch.

How to Teach Come

Start teaching the *come* command by getting your dog to pay attention to you. Hold treats in one hand and the clicker in the other, and then say your dog's name. When he looks at you, even for a moment, click and treat him, or toss a treat his way. Continue this game until he's coming over to you for a treat when you call him. If he doesn't look your way, just wait until he does.

Next, put him on a 15-foot (4.6-m) to 25-foot (7.6-m) long line and take him outside, along with your treats and clicker. Let him explore to the end of the line, and then call him. When he looks at you, encourage him to come running, showing him a treat if you have to. Click as he runs toward you, and treat when he reaches you.

If you can get someone else to help you, make a game of calling your dog to and from each person, moving farther apart as the dog understands the game. Once it's clear that he understands that coming to you results in a treat, add the word "come" to his name. Always say his name and the *come* command in a very excited and fun tone, and encourage him to come to you by patting your leg and clucking your tongue.

Teaching your Lab to sit on command can save his life in a dangerous situation.

Sit

Teaching the *sit* can save your dog's life someday, because it can stop him in his tracks if a dangerous situation presents itself.

How to Teach Sit

Start by standing with your dog standing and facing you. Hold a treat between your thumb and index finger right over his nose, and then move your hand slowly back toward his tail.

SENIOR DOG TIP

Training the Older Dog

Old dogs can learn new tricks! Clicker training is wonderful for teaching older dogs to do any new commands or tricks. Be aware that old dogs may know some commands already, but they may not know them well or may be sloppy with them. You can use the clicker to hone and sharpen commands. For example, you may want a nice, square *sit* instead of a sloppy plop-down. You can shape this behaviour by asking for small increments of change in the *sit* until you see what you want, and then only click/treat when your older dog offers that behaviour.

His head should follow the treat, and his rear should move downward into a *sit*. Click and give him the treat. If he won't sit, begin "shaping" the behaviour by clicking for approximations of the *sit*, like the rear lowering a little, then lowering more, and eventually for a full sit. Don't skimp on treats!

Next, let your dog think for a moment about how he's getting all these nice treats. He will probably offer

you a *sit* on his own to see if that's it. When he does this, click and treat. Now he'll really understand what you want and start sitting like crazy to get those treats. Add the verbal cue to sit now, and he'll come to associate the word "sit" with the behaviour. Don't add the cue too soon or you'll confuse him.

Whatever you do, don't repeat "sit sit sit sit sit sit sit sit" over and over. Your dog heard you the first time. Just wait for him to offer you the behaviour. If you have treats in your hand while using the clicker, he will definitely try to figure out what you want without having to repeat yourself.

Down

It's important to teach *down* so that you can have your dog lie down when he's being rowdy, when you need him out of the way, or when a stranger or new dog approaches him. The *down* command is a little tougher than *sit* because it's a submissive position, and some dogs won't like it. However, Labs do aim to please, so they are easy to teach just about anything.

How to Teach Down

Start with your dog in the *sit* position. Place a treat inside your hand, and let your dog smell it. Then move your hand toward the floor and slide it along the floor away from his nose. If he gets up to get the treat, put him back into the *sit* and try again. Ideally, your dog should wiggle into a *down* position as he's following the treat. Once his elbows touch the floor, click and treat (or praise and treat). Repeat, and add the verbal cue "down" once he begins to offer the behaviour on his own. Try getting him to go into a *down* from the standing position, too, using the same method once he learns how to go into the *down* from the *sit* and understands the cue.

Stay

You will need to put your dog into a solid *stay* to protect him from running off when he shouldn't and to keep him calm when a stranger or new dog approaches. *Stay* is one of the most difficult behaviours to teach because it doesn't require a dog to do anything. The other commands require action— this one requires inaction. You have to teach the *stay* in very small increments, rewarding for *stays* of one second, then two, and so on until you can get a stay of ten minutes or more. This isn't easy, and you may have setbacks, but that's okay. Just go back to step one if your dog breaks a *stay*.

How to Teach Stay

To teach this command, put your dog into a *sit* or *down* and then step in front of him, holding a flattened palm to his face. Look him in the eye and tell him, "Stay" in a firm voice. After a second, lean down and click and treat him (or praise

Your Lab may benefit from an obedience class.

and treat) and then say, "Okay," which will be your release command.

Eventually, work up to more time in the *stay*, and then vary the time in each lesson. For example, ask for 3 seconds, then 20 seconds, then 2 seconds, then 1 minute, and so on. Remember not to reward for getting up but for actually staying. Treat while the dog is in the *stay*, or he'll think that the behaviour you want is the release.

Walking Nicely on a Lead

Finally, you must teach your Lab to walk nicely on a lead. No one wants an 80-pound (36.3-kg) dog dragging her down the block. Not only is that dangerous,

but it's embarrassing. Unless you're doing competitive obedience, it's not really necessary for you to teach a strict heel at your side, but it's important to teach the dog to walk on a loose lead.

How to Teach Walking Nicely on a Lead

Start by putting your dog on the lead using a flat buckle collar. When your dog pulls, stop in your tracks and wait for him to relax and for slack to come into the lead. The second this happens, click and treat (or praise and treat), and keep walking. Repeat until the dog realises that if he pulls he won't get anywhere, but if he relaxes, he will get a treat and be able to continue walking. Use the verbal cue "let's go" when it's clear that your dog understands.

If he pulls when he sees another dog coming or something else he wants to get to, turn him around sharply, walk in the other direction, and tell him, "Let's go." Then click and treat him for coming along.

Tricks

The best tricks for Labs involve their retrieving ability. They are born to bring things back to their owners, and you can capitalise on this innate skill by teaching cute and useful tricks.

Retrieving Thrown Objects

First, begin by teaching fetch with a toy or ball. This should be easy for a Lab. Throw a ball, and then call your dog back to you. When he brings the ball back, offer him a treat (something better than what he has) and tell him to "drop it." This should come easy for your Lab.

Retrieving Stationary Objects

Once your Lab is good at retrieving things that you throw, you can train him to retrieve stationary objects, like a ringing phone, a tissue after you sneeze, or the remote control. For the tissue trick, take a box of tissues and show them to him. When he sniffs the tissue protruding from the box, click and treat. Encourage him to take the tissue—you may have to put a little peanut butter on it—and then click and treat when he puts his mouth on it. When he finally takes a tissue from the box, praise and treat him, and then ask him to "drop it" as you take it from him. Repeat this process until he understands that he's being treated for taking tissues. Now, start adding the verbal cue—sneeze (faking it, of course) and encourage him to take the tissue and give it to you.

Training might seem very difficult and time consuming, but the Lab is so intelligent and willing to please that training is actually a pleasure if you can find the right motivation for your dog. Fortunately, most Labs will work for food or a tennis ball, so you have one less challenge right off the bat. If you get frustrated, just keep at it, stay focused and positive, and above all, make it fun.

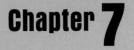

Chapter 7

In the
Doghouse

The perfect little puppy doesn't remain perfect for long, and the beautiful dog who the staff at the rescue centre said was an absolute angel probably comes with his own behavioural baggage. This chapter will help you begin to fix some of the undesired doggy behaviours that plague owners.

Barking

Dogs are territorial animals who try to protect their home and their pack. Dogs also bark because of a stimulus, such as a motorcycle going by or a squirrel in the garden. Your dog should be allowed to warn you of intruders by barking a few times, but excessive wild barking isn't acceptable

Solution

Barking is a hard habit to break once it gets started in earnest. Ideally, you will prevent barking by rewarding a puppy for quiet *sits* and *downs*. However, if the problem already exists, you'll have to come up with a training protocol to alter the dog's behaviour.

If you can interrupt the barking cycle, you have a good shot at toning the barking down. Shake a can full of pennies when your dog barks too many times—he will stop to see what the racket is and give you a chance to call him to you to get a treat. You are rewarding him for coming to you, not for barking. If he gets a treat every time he stops barking after the doorbell rings or the postman shows up, he'll eventually figure out that barking isn't as fun as eating, and he'll come looking for you to hand out the goodies.

Many dogs bark incessantly because they have separation anxiety, a set of destructive and infuriating behaviours brought about by poor socialisation or psychological trauma, such as being left at a rescue centre. If your Lab is barking nonstop when you leave the house and continues until you return, he probably has separation anxiety. If you don't know if he continues barking all day, ask your neighbours if they hear him, or leave a sound-activated recorder on while you're gone. These dogs seem to lose their minds, and not much beside your return will make

> *If you can interrupt your dog's barking cycle, you have a good chance of toning down the barking.*

the barking stop. You have to work on the separation anxiety as the root of the problem to get the barking and other behaviours to stop. Consult your vet or a behaviourist if you suspect that your dog is suffering from separation anxiety.

Chewing

Chewing is a natural behaviour that begins when a puppy is old enough to wander away from his mother and find something to put in his mouth. Puppies chew to help their puppy teeth fall out and their adult teeth to come in. They don't know that, though; they just think that chewing feels good. Because it feels good, it is considered a self-rewarding behaviour, and you're not going to be able to stop it. However, you can specify what your puppy chews. Adult dogs also like to chew, and with some training, will only chew on the toys and treats that you provide.

Solution

To prevent your Lab from chewing on inappropriate items in the first place, don't ever use an old trainer as a chew toy, or you'll be sorry when your puppy thinks that your new trainers are his, too. Use safe, hard nylon or rubber toys as acceptable chew toys. Stuffable rubber toys are great because you can add food to them to keep the puppy interested in them, not your sofa legs. Toys with squeakers are also fun. Check with your vet before giving

FAMILY-FRIENDLY TIP

Children and Aggressive Labs

Children and aggressive Labs don't mix. If your Lab has shown aggression toward children (or adults), consult a trainer or behaviourist right away. This is a large breed that can cause a lot of damage to a child. Labs are generally family dogs, but an undersocialised Lab who may have been taunted by children in the past is not going to trust children in the future.

Teach children not to approach any dog before they ask permission. If you have an aggressive Lab, keep the child and the dog separate until you can work with a trainer to resolve the issue. Instruct the child not to tease the dog and to be calm and composed when the dog is nearby. Often, dogs who are fearful of children become overly agitated when children are running and screaming.

89

your dog rawhide, pig or beef ears, or other consumable chewies. An occasional carrot or half an apple also makes a fun and low-calorie chewy treat.

The key to getting your puppy to

The Lost Dog

Finding a lost dog used to be a lot more difficult than it is today. The days of the "lost dog" posters on lampposts aren't gone, but they are dwindling as people become proactive about preparing for the worst rather than waiting until it happens.

Remember that whenever your dog is outside, he should be wearing a collar with an identification tag attached. Unfortunately, dog collars can get lost when a dog is missing, but there are two ways of permanently identifying your dog that can't get lost: a tattoo and a microchip. The tattoo is on the inside of the ear and takes just a few seconds to apply. It is a number that is individual to your dog and can be registered in a pet database. Tattoos can be altered, but the ink on the alteration will be newer and the alteration will be obvious. A microchip, however, can't be altered or removed by the average person. The chip is about the size of a grain of rice and is injected between the shoulder blades of the dog by your vet or rescue centre staff. Most vets and rescue centres have a chip scanner that reads a number off the chip. The chip is registered to your dog in the manufacturer's database or another registry.

If your dog does become lost, go out and look for him immediately, taking along as many people as you can gather. Call him and shake his treat can and squeak a toy. If you can't find him quickly, call the local dog warden and all the vets and rescue centres in the area, and tell them that you're missing your dog. Make a poster with your dog's photo, the word "reward" on it (but don't say how much to discourage a dishonest person), and a phone number (not your address), and post it all over the neighbourhood. Call breed rescue organisations in your area to tell them that you've lost a Lab. Keep up with the phone calls and the search parties. Hopefully, a good samaritan will find your dog and bring him back safely to you.

chew on things that are his, not yours, is to prevent him from getting to those items in the first place. Using a crate or isolating your puppy in a certain room and only allowing him to have items that are freely his to chew is the only way to keep a puppy from destroying your stuff. Young puppies don't understand the difference between their things and yours.

If your puppy has something in his mouth that he shouldn't have, don't make a big fuss over it, or you'll initiate a chase game and reinforce that it's fun to steal something of yours and run off with it. Instead, offer him a treat or toy in exchange for the item he has and ask him to "leave it." What you're offering should be of higher value to him than what he has; when he drops your object and takes what you're offering, praise him and remove the object. Eventually, he will learn that giving you objects results in him getting something better.

Digging

Digging is a natural and fun activity for dogs, but it's not great for your begonias. Dogs can dig a hole under the fence and escape as well, which can be very dangerous for your dog, who might get hit by a car or lost for good.

Solution

To prevent your garden from being destroyed, try offering your dog his very own sandbox filled with clean

If you catch your dog digging, call him to you and reward him if he comes.

Hiring a Behaviourist

If you have a grown Lab with issues that you can't handle, you'll need an animal behaviourist or a trainer who works with problem behaviours. This person is trained to design a protocol based on your individual dog's needs. The most important things to look for in your dog's trainer include whether or not she is compassionate, has a good bedside manner, is experienced with the Lab, uses positive training methods, does not advocate punishment, and makes you comfortable enough to ask questions and try new things.

sand or soil so that he can dig to his heart's content. Bury balls, toys, and treats in the sand, and have your dog find them. He'll soon come to realise that digging in his own box is much more rewarding than digging in your garden. Make sure to place the box in a shady area, and clean it often.

Don't make a fuss if you catch your dog digging. Instead, call him to you and reward him if he comes. If he doesn't come to you, walk calmly over to him and pull him away from the area using his collar. If he's still digging by the time you get over to him, you can tell him "no!" in a firm, sharp voice. This isn't punishment—you're just letting him know that he needs to stop what he's doing. Once you've moved him away from the hole he was digging, ask him to

do something that he knows how to do, like sit, and then praise and treat him.

You can also try having a game of fetch in the garden. The idea is to redirect your dog's energies into something else. Putting him out in the garden with a food-stuffed rubber toy helps, too. If your Lab turns out to be a chronic digger, you'll just have to keep an eye on him.

Inappropriate Toileting

It is normal for your recently housetrained puppy to have an accident if you aren't paying attention to his need to go outside. Sometimes, a puppy will have a lapse in his housetraining, and you'll have to go back to square one. This is usually more about the owner than the dog—you might have become a little less attentive and rested on the fact that your puppy knew the protocol.

Solution

To solve this problem behaviour, simply begin at your first steps in housetraining again, using praise and positive reinforcement.

You should also consider the fact that you may not be giving your dog enough opportunity to go outside. Add a toilet break to his regular routine. Become very regular with his schedule, making sure that he's eating and going out at the same times every day until he is old enough to "hold it" for a while. Finally, use a natural deodoriser on the spot in the house where he has been relieving himself. If it smells of toilet odour, he will be more likely to use that spot again in the future.

Also, don't rule out potential illness if your dog starts doing his business in the house, even though he's been reliable in his housetraining. Take your dog to the vet if you notice any such out-of-the-ordinary behaviour.

Jumping

Jumping is a big issue for many dogs, and Labs are no exception. The human face is intriguing and exciting for dogs, and they want to be as close to it as possible.

Solution

Unfortunately, the first reaction to jumping for most people is to make a fuss and push the dog back. What a fun game for the dog! Instead, you should ignore a jumping dog and take a big step back until his four feet are on the floor before you greet him. Praise him for having four on the floor, and look away and withdraw from him if he jumps, turning your attention immediately back to him when he's back on all fours. When he jumps, you can say, "Uh-uh" firmly as you back away, but don't allow the scold to be the last word. You have to find something good to praise him for immediately after.

Using the *sit* or *down* command is a perfect way to have a jumper behave himself. Train the *sit* or *down* so often that the behaviour comes as a matter of routine for the dog. Every time you have a treat in your hand, he should automatically sit. If he's sitting, he can't jump.

Self-rewarding behaviours, like jumping, are difficult to quash, and your dog might relapse in his training. That's okay—just repeat an exercise that he

With a little training and positive reinforcement, your Lab's behaviour should improve.

Aggression

Aggression in any dog is scary, but in a large dog like the Lab, it is also dangerous. Fortunately, this breed isn't known to be overly aggressive, but any undersocialised dog can become fearful and aggressive as a result. If you notice aggression toward humans—growling, baring teeth, snapping, or biting—consult a trainer or behaviourist right away. These are big warning signs. A dog should never behave aggressively toward his family or toward guests whom the family allows into the home. Dog-on-dog aggression is also dangerous and requires sessions with a trainer.

nipping by smearing the back of your hands (and your child's hands) with a very thin layer of peanut butter so that the puppy has no choice but to lick it off. Praise highly when he does, and offer treats. Get up silently and walk away if he nips, making no eye contact. If the puppy bites at your ankles or pant leg, distract him with a toy and then praise him for playing with the toy. The idea is to get him feeling happy about activities other than nipping. Don't make a fuss or yell at him, because that will either feel like a game to him or make him begin to fear you.

knows well, like the *sit* or *down*, go back to basics, and don't forget to praise and treat for a job well done.

Nipping

Puppy nipping is not aggression. Puppies nip while they're playing and to get your attention. Puppy teeth are very sharp and can hurt, though, and puppies have to learn that they should never put their teeth on human skin, no matter what.

Solution

Start by promoting "kisses" instead of

As an exercise to prevent nipping, show your dog a treat and then hold it in your closed fist. Offer him your fist, and when he nips, pull your hand back quickly and yelp loudly, as another dog would do. This will stun the puppy, because he is programmed to understand that a yelp means that he's playing too hard—this is how his littermates and mother indicated to him that his sharp little teeth weren't appreciated. Offer your hand again and repeat until your puppy gives just a sniff or a little kiss. Immediately give the treat and praise highly for the puppy's self-restraint. Remember that in training, you always want your dog to be successful at what he's doing, so make the exercise easy for him. Don't let him get frustrated. Praise and reward for small increments toward the desired behaviour, and don't expect too much too soon.

It's easiest to quell unwanted behaviours by not promoting them in the first place. For example, if you

If your puppy nips, try distracting him with a toy.

SENIOR DOG TIP

Positive Reinforcement Training

Positive reinforcement training works very well with older dogs, especially clicker training. Poor behaviour in older dogs usually comes from a lack of proper training and undersocialisation. It is a little more difficult to train a behaviour out of a dog than it is to train one in, but it is not impossible. Often, behaviour substitution is a great way to get an older dog to change his ways. For example, if you don't want your dog to scratch at the door when he wants to go out, you can train him to ring a bell hanging from the doorknob instead.

don't let your dog do something naughty, such as topple the rubbish bin, he won't learn the behaviour. Put the rubbish bin away, keep an eye on him in the garden, take him outside often to do his business, and so on. Also, remember to be consistent and fair with all of your training and retraining.

In the Doghouse

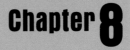

Chapter 8

Stepping Out

Labs thrive on an active social life. The Great Outdoors is a Lab's paradise, but even if you don't have a place to hike, there are plenty of activities that will keep your dog entertained. This chapter gives you some travelling tips, as well as an overview of games and sports that you can do with your active dog.

Travelling With Your Lab

Going on holiday can be stressful for both dog and owner, but it doesn't have to be that way. As pets increasingly become recognised as part of the family, they are being accepted in more places. Labs love to be with their human pack, so why not take yours along for the ride? Before deciding to take your dog along, however, take a moment to consider all the challenges that travelling with a dog entails. Does he really like to travel, and will he enjoy the trip or the destination? If your dog is unhappy, the chances are that you will be, too.

Travel Prep

The first step in getting your dog prepared for travel is to take him to your vet to get a check-up and a health certificate. Most boarding facilities will need to see proof of vaccinations and health, as will groomers should you need to take your Lab for a bath while you're away. If an accident or illness occurs, your health certificate will save valuable time if your dog has to see a vet where you're travelling. Finally, if you have a car accident or the airline loses your dog, the health certificate will help responders or employees assess and help him.

Set up a first-aid kit as described in Chapter 5. Take it with you wherever you travel, and make sure to include your dog's health certificate, pertinent medical records, medicines, and

Packing for Your Trip

When you pack for your trip, don't forget to pack for your Lab, too. Make sure to take along your dog's paperwork showing that he is up-to-date on vaccinations. Also, keep the appropriate identification tags on your dog at all times. No matter which mode of travel you're using, your dog will need food and water in containers that are unlikely to spill and are easily resealed. In addition, bring a pooper scooper, plastic bags, and a deodorising spray. In case of an emergency, bring your doggie first-aid kit.

contact phone numbers.

Lodging

Getting to and from your destination presents a host of challenges, but what to do with your dog when you get there is probably your first concern. Will your dog be able to accompany you to a majority of the sites or attractions that you plan to see? If you are going to an amusement park for a few days, does the park have a kennel on the premises where your dog will be welcome? Does it have room for your dog? What vaccinations and health certificates are required? If a kennel isn't available, is there a boarding facility nearby that can take your dog?

No matter how you and your dog get to your destination, it's essential to confirm beforehand that the lodging you'll potentially be using is dog friendly. Many pet-friendly hotels are available, especially near popular destinations. Call ahead to ask about extra pet fees or deposits, and ask about the rules regarding where the dog can walk and if he's allowed in the lobby.

Car Travel

In general, Labradors have a lot of experience with car rides from an early age, because most people take them to parks, lakes, camping, and at the very least, to the vet and pet shop. For a Lab who has little experience with car travel, warm him up to the idea of a long car trip with a few practice runs. Put your Lab in the car and turn on the engine, and then offer him treats and allow him out of the car. Repeat until he's happy jumping into the car on his own. Next, drive around for a few minutes, treating as you go, and increasing driving time as your dog becomes comfortable with it. Then, choose a fun destination, like a park, and reward your dog with a treat or playtime. On these practice runs, visit a pet store that allows animals inside, and have your dog meet other people and other dogs.

Bring along the dog's first-aid kit or at least a remedy for an upset

To desensitise your Lab to the car, first allow him to just sit in the vehicle.

FAMILY-FRIENDLY TIP

Travelling With Labs and Children

When travelling with a Labrador and children, make sure that the children do not increase the Lab's stress level. You'll be watching the road when you're driving, and you'll have to trust that your children are being kind to the dog in the back with them. Children should understand that they should let a dog sleep and not expect to have rowdy playtime in the car. Of course, children can pet the dog as long as they don't excite him.

stomach caused by car-sickness. During the trip, your dog should get sufficient food and water at rest stops. He should also receive frequent toilet breaks, and don't forget to bring plastic bags to clean up after him. You might also want to bring a deodorising spray, depending on where you're planning on staying or if your dog is prone to getting sick in the car. Your vet can recommend something for car-sickness before the trip that can be taken shortly before getting in the car to avoid any unpleasantness in the first place.

While in the car, your dog should have some protection against injury in case of an accident. If your Lab is used to a crate, it can provide the same sense of safety when bungee-corded into the backseat of the car. Or purchase a dog harness or car seat that works with the seatbelt to keep your dog from flying forward if you have to brake suddenly or if an accident occurs. Remember, an object in motion will stay in motion, even if the car stops. Your Lab will become a flying object in an accident, which is especially dangerous for any humans in the car. Also, dogs should *never* travel in the open bed of a pickup truck. They could easily fall out or become injured while sliding around. A dog in the bed of a truck is vulnerable to inclement weather and debris that might blow off other cars or trucks.

Keep your dog at a comfortable temperature to avoid heatstroke and hypothermia. Never leave him in the car alone in even mildly warm temperatures, even if you open a window.

Airline Travel

Air travel for dogs was rarely undertaken in the UK, but with the PETS passport scheme it is becoming more commonplace. If you are travelling by plane, speak with the airline about what information it will need to allow your dog on board. Make sure that your dog has a comfortable crate with a water bottle attached to the front, and give him a safe chew toy when you leave him in the airline's care. Be careful when flying with pets during extreme weather.

Some airlines recommend that pets be sedated before being stowed on the plane. This really depends on the dog and should be discussed with your vet. Evidence suggests that being sedated while flying can lead to increased risk of death and injury for the dog. It decreases his oxygen intake and his reaction time if something were to happen—for example, if the crate were dropped. Under sedation, dogs are less able to protect themselves from being jostled around. However, some dogs really hate travelling, and sedation makes the trip less troublesome for those individuals. If sedation seems necessary, consult with your vet about giving the dog a lesser amount of a sedative just to calm him without knocking him out.

Many Labs excel as guides for the blind.

Kennelling and Dog Sitting

If travelling with your dog isn't possible on certain trips, you will have to find someone to care for him while you're gone. Your choices are a boarding kennel or a live-in or visiting pet sitter.

Choosing a boarding kennel is similar to choosing a vet; you have to make sure that you're putting your dog into a quality place. Visit several kennels in your area before choosing one. Find out what paperwork dogs need to be able to stay there. Ask about the vet whom the kennel has on call and if she is available 24 hours a day. Make sure that someone at the kennel is there at all times to speak with you on the phone in case you want to check up on how your dog is doing.

SENIOR DOG TIP

Travelling With an Older Dog

Travelling with an older dog is not much different from travelling with younger dogs, except that the senior dog requires a slightly gentler touch. Older dogs need a comfier place to lie, since their joints may be more delicate and achy. Older dogs also need to stop for bathroom breaks more frequently and might need some extra help getting into and out of the car.

Professional pet sitters are people who have trained to watch animals and are bonded and accredited with a pet-sitting organisation. You can also ask for references. Professional pet sitters are acquainted with pet health and training, and they may have taken courses about all aspects of pet care, including disaster preparation and planning. Many have insurance as well.

Sports

Your Lab can participate and excel in a variety of sports that require beauty, speed, grace, training, or instinct. Here is a list of just a few competitive dog sports you can do with your Lab.

Agility

In agility trials, a dog runs off-lead through a series of obstacles, ideally faster than all the other dogs in the competition. Dogs must finish the course in a specified time without missing an obstacle or knocking over a jump pole. Agility trials are held by agility organisations and are sanctioned by the Kennel Club.

Canine Freestyle

Canine freestyle is a dancing competition in which owners and dogs create a dance routine and perform it to music. It might sound a little unusual, but it's a lot of fun and promotes bonding between dog and owner. Freestyle is beautiful to watch, and it is a great way to reinforce training skills.

Dock Jumping

In this all-American sport, a dog runs down a dock and jumps in after a floating bumper, rubber duck, or other toy. It's kind of like the long jump in the Olympics—the dog who jumps the farthest wins. This is a perfect sport for Labradors, who love to fetch and swim.

Dog Shows (Conformation)

Not all Labs are show dogs, but if

your Labrador Retriever is registered with the Kennel Club, is intact (not neutered), is well socialised with other dogs, is well trained and compatible with humans, is sound and healthy, and meets the breed standard for Labrador Retrievers, he is eligible to compete in KC conformation shows. If you think you may be interested in showing, contact the KC and complete the appropriate paperwork.

Showing in conformation shows is a lot of fun, and you'll get to meet a lot of other owners who are also passionate about the breed. You'll have a lot of competition, because Labs tend to be registered in large numbers. Attend a couple of shows before you consider entering your dog, and leave your dog at home when you go. Most shows don't allowed unregistered dogs to enter the show grounds.

Flying Disk

Flying disk competitions are an American invention and have several events: distance, time trial, accuracy, and freestyle. Distance tests how far the dog can run and then jump to catch a flying disk. Accuracy tests how often the dog catches the flying disk. The time trial sees what the dog can do in a given amount of time. Freestyle is a routine that owner and dog perform that involves catches and tricks. Points are scored based on how difficult the tricks are and how well the dog catches the flying disk.

In agility trials, a dog must complete a series of obstacles as quickly as possible.

Sports and Safety

Like humans, dogs need to ease their way into a workout. Before a Labrador begins training for a sport, he should have a check-up to make sure that he's healthy. Speak with your vet about your dog's diet. With added exercise, your Lab may need more food or different nutrients to compensate for all the energy he will burn. When starting to train for a sport, begin slowly, and gradually work your dog up to the level the sport requires. Start with a warm-up before practice or a competition, and make sure that your dog receives enough water throughout. During competition, ensure that your dog is not too hot or cold and that he does not get too much sun.

You and your Lab run from obstacle to obstacle and receive directions about which exercise to perform at each station. You are allowed to communicate as much as you please with your dog.

Obedience competitions are generally quieter, more formal and require greater accuracy.

Retriever Field Trials

In this sport, which tests the Lab's stamina and memory, a dog must retrieve downed game. This generally involves a combination of straightforward retrieves, in which the dog knows where the game is; "blind" retrieves, in which the dog must find the game in the field just using his nose; or multiple retrieves, in which the dog must locate and retrieve several game objects.

Retriever Hunting Trials

In this trial, a dog is judged based on how he controls himself before and during a hunt and how he honours another dog's retrieve. Obstacles and decoys are also placed that simulate a natural hunt so that the dog has to think to get to his game.

Tracking

Tracking tests a dog's ability to follow human scent through a series of terrains. In the UK this is incorporated

Obedience

Obedience competitions sanctioned by the Kennel Club are open to all dogs registered with the Kennel Club of at least six months of age. Dogs perform various obedience commands given by their owner. Labs are great at obedience! Don't worry about being a beginner to the sport; you'll be placed in the beginner's class until your dog is more experienced.

Rally-0

This new American sport is like obedience competition but less formal.

in Working Trials. In the US, Tracking is a discipline in its own right, where dogs can earn Tracking titles. Labradors excel at finding and following scents.

Games

So what if you don't want to get involved in organised sports? Although they are fun, they are also time consuming, and a lot of loving dog owners don't have that kind of time to spend. Your Lab will be just as thrilled with everyday activities that are closer to home, don't require much training, and best of all, are done with you by his side.

Hiking and Camping

Hiking and camping are as natural for a Lab as breathing. This outdoorsy dog loves romping through the woods, smelling all the wonderful scents, and jumping into streams and ponds. Just as you'd bring water and a snack for a day of hiking, you have to bring dog supplies too. Pack a bag for your dog, including water and a foldable canvas bowl, a few treats (great for luring him out of the water), and tweezers in case he gets something stuck in his feet or nose. Don't forget flea and tick protection (whatever your vet recommends). Also, when you get home from a hike or camping, groom your dog closely, looking for ticks.

Hot Dog Dive

If you want to stay closer to home but still want your Lab to have a tiring romp, fill up a baby pool with water and then slice up a couple of hot dogs and toss them into the pool. Toss a couple of tennis balls in there, too, and be prepared to get soaked—don't wear your best clothes on hot dog diving day!

Games and sports aren't just about fun and prizes; they also provide you and your Lab with important bonding time. Going on walks counts, too, as does a simple game of fetch, a game in which Labs excel. Remember, this social dog likes to expand his horizons, so try to take him with you anywhere that allows dogs.

Playing games with your Lab will strengthen the bond between the two of you.

Resources

Associations and Organisations

Breed Clubs

American Kennel Club (AKC)
5580 Centerview Drive
Raleigh, NC 27606
Telephone: (919) 233-9767
Fax: (919) 233-3627
E-mail: info@akc.org
www.akc.org

Canadian Kennel Club (CKC)
89 Skyway Avenue, Suite 100
Etobicoke, Ontario M9W 6R4
Telephone: (416) 675-5511
Fax: (416) 675-6506
E-mail: information@ckc.ca
www.ckc.ca

Federation Cynologique Internationale (FCI)
Secretariat General de la FCI
Place Albert 1er, 13
B – 6530 Thuin, Belqique
www.fci.be

The Kennel Club
1 Clarges Street
London W1J 8AB
Telephone: 0870 606 6750
Fax: 0207 518 1058
www.the-kennel-club.org.uk

United Kennel Club (UKC)
100 E. Kilgore Road
Kalamazoo, MI 49002-5584
Telephone: (269) 343-9020
Fax: (269) 343-7037
E-mail: pbickell@ukcdogs.com
www.ukcdogs.com

Pet Sitters

National Association of Registered Pet Sitters
www.dogsit.com

UK Pet Sitters
Telephone: 01902 41789
www.ukpetsitter.com

Dog Services UK
www.dogservices.co.uk

Rescue Organisations and Animal Welfare Groups

British Veterinary AssociationAnimal Welfare Foundation (BVA AWF)
7 Mansfield Street
London W1G 9NQ
Telephone: 0207 636 6541
Fax: 0207 436 2970
Email: bva-awf@bva.co.uk
www.bva-awf.org.uk/about

Royal Society for the Prevention of Cruelty to Animals (RSPCA)
Telephone: 0870 3335 999
Fax: 0870 7530 284
www.rspca.org.uk

Scottish Society for the Prevention of Cruelty to Animals (SSPCA)
Braehead Mains, 603 Queensferry Road
Edinburgh EH4 6EA
Telephone: 0131 339 0222
Fax: 0131 339 4777
Email: enquiries@scottishspca.org
www.scottishspca.org/about

Sports

Agility Club UK
www.agilityclub.co.uk

British Flyball Association
PO Box 109, Petersfield GU32 1XZ
Telephone: 01753 620110
Fax: 01726 861079
Email: bfa@flyball.org.uk
www.flyball.org.uk

Canine Freestyle Federation, Inc.
Secretary: Brandy Clymire
E-Mail: secretary@canine-freestyle.org
www.canine-freestyle.org

International Agility Link (IAL)
Global Administrator: Steve Drinkwater
E-mail: yunde@powerup.au
www.agilityclick.com/~ial

World Canine Freestyle Organisation
P.O. Box 350122, Brooklyn, NY 11235-2525
Telephone: (718) 332-8336
www.worldcannefreestyle.org

Therapy
Pets As Therapy
3 Grange Farm Cottages, Wycombe Road,
Saunderton, Princes Risborough
Bucks HP27 9NS
Telephone: 0870 977 0003
Fax: 0870 706 2562
www.petsastherapy.org

Therapy Dogs International (TDI)
88 Bartley Road
Flanders, NJ 07836
Telephone: (973) 252-9800
Fax: (973) 252-7171
E-mail: tdi@gti.net
www.tdi-dog.org

Training and Behaviour
Association of Pet Dog Trainers (APDT)
PO Box 17
Kempsford GL7 4W7
Telephone: 01285 810811

Association of Pet Behaviour Counsellors
PO Box 46
Worcester WR8 9YS
Telephone: 01386 751151
Fax: 01386 750743
Email: info@apbc.org.uk
www.apbc.org.uk

Veterinary and Health Resources
Association of British Veterinary Acupuncturists (ABVA)
66A Easthorpe, Southwell
Nottinghamshire NG25 0HZ
Email: jonnyboyvet@hotmail.com
www.abva.co.uk

Association of Chartered Physiotherapists Specialising in Animal Therapy (ACPAT)
52 Littleham Road
Exmoouth, Devon EX8 2QJ
Telephone/Fax: 01395 270648
Email: bexsharples@hotmail.com
www.acpat.org.uk

British Association of Homoeopathic Veterinary Surgeons
Alternative Veterinary Medicine Centre
Chinham House, Stanford in the Vale
Oxfordshire SN7 8NQ
Email: enquiries@bahvs.com
www.bahvs.com

British Association of Veterinary Opthalmologists (BAVO)
Email: hjf@vetspecialists.co.uk
Email: secretary@bravo.org.uk
www.bravo.oprg.uk

British Small Animal Veterinary Association (BSAVA)
Woodrow House, 1 Telford Way
Waterwells Business Park
Quedgley, Gloucester GL2 2AB
Telephone: 01452 726700
Email: customerservices@bsava.com
www.bsava.com

British Veterinary Association (BVA)
7 Mansfield Street, London W1G 9NQ
Telephone: 020 7636 6541
E-mail: bvahq@bva.co.uk
www.bva.co.uk

British Veterinary Hospitals Association (BHVA)
Station Bungalow, Main Road, Stockfield
Northumberland NE43 7HJ
Telephone: 07966 901619
Email: office@bvha.org.uk
www.BVHA.org.uk

Royal College of Veterinary Surgeons (RCVS)
Belgravia House, 62-64 Horseferry Road
London SW1P 2AF
Telephone: 0207 222 2001
Email: admin@rcvs.org.uk
www.rcvs.org.uk

Publications

Books
Anderson, Teoti. *The Super Simple Guide to Housetraining*. Neptune City: TFH Publications, 2004.

Morgan, Diane. *Good Dogkeeping*. Neptune City: TFH Publications, 2005.
Morgan, Diane. *The Labrador Retriever*. Neptune City: TFH Publications, 2005.

Yin, Sophia, DVM. *How to Behave So Your Dog Behaves*. Neptune City: TFH Publications, 2004.

Tennant, Colin. *Mini Encyclopedia Dog Training & Behaviour*. Dorking: Interpet Publishing, 2005.

Evans, Jim. *What If My Dog....?* Dorking: Interpet Publishing, 2006.

Newpapers and Magazines
Dog World Ltd
Somerfield House
Wotton Road, Ashford
Kent TN23 6LW
Telephone: 01233 621877
Fax: 01233 645669

Dogs Monthly
Ascot House, High Street,
Ascot, Berkshire SL5 7JG
Telephone: 0870 730 8433
Fax: 0870 730 8431
E-mail: admin@rtc-associates.freeserve.co.uk
www.corsini.co.uk/dogsmonthly

Dogs Today
Town Mill, Bagshot Road
Chobham, Surrey GU24 8BZ
Telephone: 01276 858880
Fax: 01276 858860
Email: enquiries@dogstodaymagazine.co.uk
www.dogstodaymagazine.co.uk

Kennel Gazette
Kennel Club, 1 Clarges Street
London W1J 8AB
Telephone: 0870 606 6750
Fax: 0207 518 1058
www.the-kennel-club.co.uk

K9 Magazine
21 High Street
Warsop, Nottinghamshire NG20 0AA
Telephone: 0870 011 4114
Fax: 0870 706 4564
Email: mail@k9magazine.com
www.k9magazine.com

Our Dogs
Our Dogs Publishing
5 Oxford Road, Station Approach
Manchester M60 1SX
www.ourdogs.co.uk

Your Dog
Roebuck House
33 Broad Street
Stamford
Lincolnshire PE9 1RB
Telephone: 01780 766199
Fax: 01780 766416

Index

Note: Boldface numbers indicate illustrations; an italic *t* indicates a table.

111

Index

Dedication

This book is dedicated to Pepper and Ozzie, the perfection of doginess.

Acknowledgements

The author would like to thank T.F. H. and her editor, Stephanie Fornino, for her kind patience and editorial expertise.

About the Author

Nikki Moustaki, MA, is a dog trainer in New York City where she lives with her two Schnauzers. She is the author of several books on dogs and dog training, has written for many national magazines, and also writes extensively on bird care, training, and behaviour. Nikki has been featured on television and radio shows and currently hosts www.dogandpuppy.com.